Peter
Keys to Following Jesus

Tim Gray

Ignatius Press–Augustine Institute

San Francisco   Greenwood Village, CO

Ignatius Press Distribution
1915 Aster Rd.
Sycamore, IL 60178
Tel: (800) 651-1531
www.ignatius.com

Augustine Institute
6160 S. Syracuse Way, Suite 310
Greenwood Village, CO 80111
Tel: (866) 767-3155
www.augustineinstitute.org

Cover Design: Devin Schadt

Cover Art:
Saint Peter
by Pompeo Girolamo Batoni (1708–1787)
Basildon Park, Berkshire, UK
© National Trust Photographic Library/John Hammond
The Bridgeman Art Library

Copyright © 2016 Ignatius Press, San Francisco,
and the Augustine Institute, Greenwood Village, CO
All rights reserved.
ISBN: 978-1-62164-070-7
Library of Congress Control Number 2016946129
Printed in Canada

Contents

Foreword

The overriding purpose of this book is to give a deep insight into the person of Peter within the time, places, and cultures in which he encountered Jesus and led the apostolic Church. It is also an attempt to set out the framework for a deeper personal encounter with Jesus, a more dynamic relationship with the Church, and a general plan for entering into discipleship and the New Evangelization.

Dr. Gray synthesizes insights of mind, heart, and spirit through his many scholarly and artistic interests and studies. Combining a remarkable knowledge of the language, geography, art, and ancient sites of both Israel and Rome, he weaves together the scriptural, traditional, and archaeological evidence of the life of Peter—giving us a deep personal insight into the head Apostle—as if we were really there.

One of Dr. Gray's greatest strengths is his ability to unfold the deep historical, linguistic, cultural, spiritual, and scriptural richness of the many cryptic expressions and names found in the passages describing the first Apostle. As Dr. Gray considers each word or phrase, we see not only the Old Testament context out of which these words were spoken, but their deep spiritual significance—literally and metaphorically. As he considers each major stage in the life of Peter, he moves effortlessly between etymological and grammatical studies, Old Testament history and prophecy, description of geographical sites and artistic masterpieces from the Catholic Tradition, and a deep spiritual appreciation of the Lordship of Jesus, and a seeming personal familiarity with Peter himself.

Two of the most revealing chapters are those on Peter's primacy, in which Dr. Gray's elucidation of the text reveals not only Jesus's trust in Peter, a man of many flaws, but also his desire to establish a Church with Peter as "the rock"—the foundation—with Jesus himself as the new temple. Dr. Gray's study of the pertinent passages gives a solid foundation upon which to trust the Church as the living Body of Christ.

Though this book is not written as a formal apologetic for Petrine primacy, it presents compelling reasons for believing this to be the intention of Jesus in selecting Peter as the first Apostle and appointing him as his "prime minister" (by giving him the keys to the kingdom). I found Dr. Gray's use of the phrase "prime minister" to refer to the "appointed holder of the keys to the kingdom" to be exceedingly enlightening—and also found his justification for doing so to be quite convincing. Dr. Gray begins by showing the parallels between the Davidic kingdom and the kingdom of Jesus. Just as David believed himself to be the steward of *God's* kingdom (in his absence), so also Peter was to be the *steward* of Jesus's divine kingdom in *his* absence (see 1 Chr 29:10–11, 23).

Dr. Gray develops this theme by showing its presence in the Genesis narrative, where Joseph was made steward "over the house" ("*ha al bayyit*") of Pharaoh, giving Joseph authority over the kingdom in Pharaoh's absence.

The final and most telling parallel occurs in the Book of Isaiah (22:18–22) in which Isaiah delivers an oracle to Shebna who was appointed prime minister of the house—the kingdom—of Judah by King Hezekiah. Shebna proved himself unfaithful by not trusting in God and anticipating Israel's fall to the Assyrians. Assuming he would die at the hands of the Assyrians, he constructed an elaborate tomb for himself. Since Shebna had not trusted God, God replaced him as prime minister by sending Isaiah the prophet with an oracle against Shebna and an appointment of Eliakim as his replacement:

> I will thrust you from your office, and you will be cast down from your station. In that day I will call my servant Eli'akim the son of Hilki'ah, and I will clothe him with your robe, and will bind your belt on him, and will commit your authority to his hand; and he shall be a father to the inhabitants of Jerusalem and to the *house of Judah. And I will place on his [Eliakim's] shoulder the key of the house of David; he shall open, and none shall shut; and he shall shut, and non shall open.* (Is 22:19–22, emphasis added)

Compare the last italicized line from the above oracle of Isaiah appointing Eliakim as new prime minister of the kingdom of Judah ("the house of Judah") and the words of Jesus to appoint Peter as head of the Church: "I will give you the keys of the kingdom of heaven, and whatever you bind on earth shall be bound in heaven, and whatever you loose on earth shall be loosed in heaven" (Mt 16:19). The parallelism is so striking that it cannot be thought that this passage from Isaiah was not in the mind of Matthew—and Jesus—in using such words of appointment. If this is the case, then one cannot separate the intention of Jesus from the rest of the oracle of Isaiah that shows the keys to the kingdom are connected with an *office* and with the *authority of God* in that office. As Isaiah notes, "I will thrust you from your *office*, and you will be cast down from your *station* ... and I will commit your *authority* to his hand."

Though I have read many accounts of the significance of the "keys to the kingdom," I consider Dr. Gray's analysis to be one of the finest because it shows not only Jesus's intention to appoint Peter as head of the Apostles and head of the Church, but also to create an *office* of prime minister with his *divine authority* to be used in his absence. Inasmuch as Jesus and Matthew had the oracle of Isaiah in mind (which seems quite likely), then Jesus initiated an office of prime minister with divine authority—appointing Peter as the first holder of that office.

As noted above, Dr. Gray has a multifaceted purpose in writing this book, beyond establishing Peter's position and office within the Church, which is the temple of Jesus's body. One of those purposes is to impart a theology of discipleship and evangelization based on seven interactions between Jesus and Peter (and sometimes the other disciples). Each interaction comes after a failure on the part of Peter (or the disciples) to understand or act properly. Dr. Gray sees these occasions of failure as intentional learning moments—not only for Peter, but for anyone who aspires to be like him in discipleship and evangelization.

1. In one of Peter's finest hours, when he distinguishes himself from the other Apostles and comes to meet

Jesus on the water, Peter takes his eyes off of Jesus and looks at the rough waters beneath him, and begins to sink. Dr. Gray takes Jesus's instruction to Peter as a primary tenet of discipleship: be constant, childlike, and bold in your faith; keep your eyes fixed on Jesus; and remember that fear undermines faith.

2. Immediately after witnessing the miracle of the loaves and fishes, the Apostles begin to feel quite proud of Jesus's success, at which point Jesus warns them to avoid the leaven of the Pharisees. Dr. Gray explains that *leaven* means "pride" or "puffed up" and even "corruption," from which he draws the lesson that true disciples should not seek success and prestige in the world (the leaven of the Pharisees) but rather imitate the humble service of Jesus.

3. After witnessing the miracle of the loaves and fishes, it seems incredible that the Apostles would be concerned about not having enough bread to eat. Jesus uses the occasion to tell them to be careful about spiritual blindness—"hardness of heart" which prevents them from seeing and believing in the power of Jesus to take care of them and lead them. Dr. Gray advises that true disciples possess this confidence in Jesus, and that when we become overly concerned about needs or things of the world, we become spiritually blind and apostolically ineffective.

4. After Jesus commissions Peter, giving him the office of prime minister, he tells his disciples that he must

suffer, die, and be raised on the third day. Peter responds by saying, "God forbid, Lord! This shall never happen to you" (Mt 16:22). Jesus rebukes Peter by saying, "Get behind me, Satan [adversary]! You are a hindrance to me; for you are not on the side of God, but of men" (Mt 16:23). Dr. Gray advises that even though disciples are given great authority, Jesus is the king, and we must follow *his* way, which is the way of the Cross. True disciples should expect the Cross—not only because their word will be resisted by the world but also because it is the way in which God's providence brings about the kingdom of love.

5. In the Garden of Gethsemane, Jesus takes Peter, James, and John to a place by themselves, and then goes ahead of them to pray. He tells them, "Watch and pray" (Mt 26:41), but every time he returns, they are asleep. Dr. Gray advises that true disciples will etch these words in their hearts, being vigilant in prayer and following the example of Jesus, their master.

6. As Jesus is taken from the Garden of Gethsemane to the house of Caiaphas, Luke says that "Peter followed at a distance" (Lk 22:54), which seems to have weakened his resolve, culminating in his threefold denial of Jesus. Dr. Gray advises that true disciples cannot afford to follow Jesus's way of discipleship at a distance, that is, to be a comfortable disciple. Too much comfort—attachment to the world and detachment from the way of Jesus—will weaken our resolve and culminate in failures of discipleship.

7. After Peter denies Jesus three times, Jesus invites Peter to acknowledge his love, effectively reconciling him and restoring him to his position as head of the Church. The lesson here is that true disciples can always count on Jesus to invite them back into his life and ministry even after failures—even colossal failures like Peter's denials. Note that all the above lessons of discipleship are derived from failures of Peter or the disciples to understand or act properly. Jesus uses these failings to teach his disciples about good discipleship, but there is also another message. Even if we fail at being good disciples, Jesus, through the power of the Holy Spirit, working in the immensity of his providential plan, can restore us, teach us through our failures, and after our chastening, make us into even better disciples. Whatever we do, we cannot allow ourselves to be discouraged. We must have the same childlike heart of Peter to hear the invitation of Jesus and accept his reconciling love when we have failed, even colossally.

Dr. Gray invites all of us to follow the example of Peter in discipleship and evangelization. Through his interpretation of the interactions between Jesus and Peter, he encourages us to courageously bear witness to the effects of Jesus in *our personal lives*. We can use this personal testimony to show further the holiness, goodness, love, and risen presence of Jesus. As with Peter, this personal witness will incite some to belief—and when it does, we must hasten to invite them to

Baptism, repentance, and the ultimate dignity of discipleship
within the Church.

Fr. Robert Spitzer
Feast of the Chair of St. Peter
February 22, 2016

Chapter 1

Put Out into the Deep:
The Making of an Apostle

When we read the New Testament, it is easy to see that Peter, in many ways, is the model disciple. There is much to be learned from how he interacted with Jesus and the other Apostles. One thing that makes him especially appealing is his approachability as an everyday kind of man. Peter was a simple, hardworking, ordinary person. Yet, when he encountered Jesus, he was called out of his own "little" story into a much bigger story—the story of Jesus Christ himself.

Peter, as we all know, was a fisherman, and fishing was hard, strenuous work, so he would have been tough. His face would have been sunburned, his hands would have been calloused, and his fingernails would have been dirty. He wasn't an educated man like the rabbis and scribes, and yet he powerfully proclaimed the Word of God. This aspect of Peter is wonderfully illustrated in the scene from the Acts of the Apostles (*cf.* 4:13) in which Peter, following his arrest, preached courageously before the Sanhedrin. We are told that the members of the Sanhedrin were amazed at his preaching because he was an uneducated man. This, however, would have been unsurprising to Paul, who said,

"Consider your call, brethren; not many of you were wise according to worldly standards, not many were powerful, not many were of noble birth; but God chose what is foolish in the world to shame the wise, God chose what is weak in the world to shame the strong" (1 Cor 1:26–27).

The Qualifications of Peter and All Apostles

We see time and time again that God chooses people like Peter. He doesn't call the equipped; he equips the called. That should be a great consolation and encouragement to us—to know that God chooses people who don't have the perfect background and preparation. He calls people who have a heart open to him and a willingness to do his will. That is all it takes. It's that *fiat*, that willingness to say "yes," that we see with the call of Peter.

Peter could be bold and impetuous at times, and it seems he often had his foot in his mouth. In moments of weakness, he was also a sinful man. Most memorably, he even betrayed Jesus in the Lord's direst hour. Yet, he repented and wept bitterly out of true sorrow and love. In fact, it is this tremendous love of Christ that makes him a great model, not only in how we should follow Christ but also in how we should repent. All of these human characteristics have made Peter especially beloved by Christians throughout the ages—beginning in the early Church.

In the Acts of the Apostles, we read how Peter led the apostolic Church. For example, Peter saw the need to elect someone to fill the office left vacant by Judas, and he guided the Church in her very first decision after Christ's Ascension.

> In those days Peter stood up among the brethren (the company of
> persons was in all about a hundred and twenty), and said ... "It is
> written in the book of Psalms, 'Let his habitation become desolate,
> and let there be no one to live in it'; and 'His office let another take.'
> So one of the men who have accompanied us during all the time
> that the Lord Jesus went in and out among us, beginning from the
> baptism of John until the day when he was taken up from us—one
> of these men must become with us a witness to his resurrection."
> (Acts 1:15, 20–22)

By choosing the criteria to be used in electing an Apostle, Peter was telling the early Christian community that the most important qualification for an Apostle was how much time that person had spent with Jesus. Even today this is the earmark of a disciple of Christ. For the first Christians, this meant time spent with Christ *in person*; for us, this means time spent with him in prayer, in worship, and in adoration. Peter himself fulfilled this key qualification of an Apostle perhaps better than anyone else. As the head of Christ's inner circle of Apostles, he had a close relationship with Christ and was an intimate witness of Christ's life and teachings.

Peter's Proximity to Christ in Early Christian Art

This close relationship between Peter and Christ was so apparent that it was often reflected in early Christian art. One example can be found in the depictions carved into the sarcophagus of a wealthy, Christian woman, dated about AD 300. The beautiful artwork on the sarcophagus represents the style of Christian art that existed in Western Europe before Christianity was legalized by Constantine in AD 313. The sarcophagus, which illustrates events from the life of Jesus, shows Peter right next to Jesus in every single scene.

Curiously, these illustrations of Peter depict him with curly hair and a curly beard—the quintessential representation of Peter in early Christian art. The reason for this particular depiction of Peter goes back to the Roman custom of representing the emperor in art. Every town or village or person who wanted to have an image of the emperor had to copy the image that was approved by Rome itself. The idea was that everyone in the Roman Empire would be able to identify the image of the emperor because it was always the same. The early Christians adopted this practice in their own art. They wanted every Christian throughout the empire to be able to recognize Peter, Paul, Jesus, etc., whenever they were depicted.

It is also important to note that the depictions of Jesus are not what we are accustomed to in later Christian art. Here, as was the artistic custom in the early Church, Jesus appears as a young man without a beard. In Roman art, a beardless youth signified divinity. You can see this with artistic renditions of the Roman emperor. For example, Caesar Augustus—as with all images of the emperors—always appears clean shaven. It's not until Hadrian, who reigned AD 117–138, that we see an emperor depicted with a beard. Just as the emperor was considered divine, Christ—who is the Son of God and, therefore, truly divine—appears youthful and clean shaven to signify his divinity, his Resurrection from the dead, and eternal life.

Sarcophagus of Sabinas, Vatican Museum

Beginning at the far right of the sarcophagus, we see the gospel scene of the hemorrhaging woman who was healed by touching Jesus's garment—and Peter is standing right next to him. The Gospel tells us that Jesus stopped and asked, "Who was it that touched me?" (Lk 21:45). Peter, who was attempting, somewhat unsuccessfully, to keep the crowd at arm's length, seemed a little offended and answered, "Master, the multitudes surround you and press upon you!" (ibid.).

The next scene on the sarcophagus shows the paralytic man who was healed by Christ. Once again, Peter is standing beside Jesus, watching him carefully. We'll examine the story of the paralytic more closely in the next chapter. The following scene depicts the blind man who was healed by Jesus. While Jesus is touching the eyes of the man, we notice Peter standing right beside him. Peter is constantly there, scene after scene, peering over Jesus's shoulder.

The main illustration on the sarcophagus is taken from the Wedding at Cana. We see servants with the containers of water that have been changed into wine. Of course, Peter is there again looking over Christ's shoulder. Then, directly in the center of the sarcophagus, there is a woman, depicted in a gesture of prayer. This represents the woman who was buried in the sarcophagus. Her hands are outstretched, demonstrating that she is asking for prayers of intercession. It's interesting that in AD 300, we have this example of a Christian seeking prayers after she has passed away. That the artist placed this petitioning woman next to the Wedding at Cana scene seems to identify her with the Blessed Virgin Mary, who interceded with Christ to change the water into wine. Perhaps this woman had a great devotion to Our Lady. We can't be sure, but the placement of her in this scene is rather suggestive of Marian devotion.

As we continue to look at the sarcophagus, we see the gospel episode where Peter is arrested. Later, we see him in prison along with two guards who are drinking water from the rock that Peter struck. This represents the Baptism of the guards who converted after having been evangelized by Peter. These artistic depictions of Peter, most of which show him looking over Christ's shoulder, are drawn from the Gospels themselves. Peter is mentioned twenty-five times in Matthew's Gospel, twenty-five in Mark's, thirty in Luke's, and thirty-nine in John's. And almost every time he is mentioned, he is right next to Jesus.

This close proximity to Jesus gave Peter a unique perspective, and the study of his life opens up for us a window into the Person, life, teaching, and mission of Jesus Christ. Because of this, we can say that the closer we get to Peter, the closer we get to Christ himself. While this close relationship of Peter to Christ is one reason for us to study Peter in more depth, there is another reason that stands out above the others. Peter is the bridge for our understanding of the relationship between Christ and his Church. He becomes that bridge when Jesus turns to Peter and says, "You are Peter, and on this rock I will build my church, and the gates of Hades shall not prevail against it. I will give you the keys of the kingdom of heaven, and whatever you bind on earth shall be bound in heaven, and whatever you loose on earth shall be loosed in heaven" (Mt 16:18–19). Appointed by Christ himself, Peter was the first leader of the Church community, the "Vicar of Christ" on earth.

In today's society, there is often a mistaken sense of self-independence that says we don't need organized religion or we don't need the Church. This would have been incomprehensible to Peter and the Apostles and, as you will see in our studies, to Christ himself. Recently, there was a book published with a title like *How to Be Christian without Going to Church*. Ideas such as this demonstrate that there is something of an identity crisis as to what the Church is supposed to be. This makes it very important to go back to the very origins of the Church, and back to that rock upon which Christ built his Church. By doing this, we will understand better what Jesus intended for the Church, why we need the Church, and why the Church is a firm foundation for our faith.

The Call of Three Apostles

In the Gospel of John, we read about the first encounters of three future Apostles with Jesus Christ. John the Baptist had summoned Israel to repentance and baptism in the River Jordan. While he was preaching in the Jordanian wilderness, the scribes and Pharisees sought him out to learn who he was. John told them that he was not the messiah but that someone greater than he was coming in the near future, during his own lifetime.

> "I baptize with water; but among you stands one whom you do not know, even he who comes after me, the thong of whose sandal I am not worthy to untie." (Jn 1:26)

The Gospel then goes on to tell us that Jesus came and was baptized by John, who bore witness to him, saying:

> "I saw the Spirit descend as a dove from heaven, and it remained on him. I myself did not know him; but he who sent me to baptize with water said to me, 'He on whom you see the Spirit descend and remain, this is he who baptizes with the Holy Spirit.' And I have seen and have borne witness that this is the Son of God." (Jn 1:32–34)

The next day, John was standing with two of his disciples when he saw Christ. John pointed him out to his disciples and said, "Behold, the Lamb of God!" (Jn 1:26). The disciples heard him and then followed Jesus. Jesus turned to the two and asked them, "What do you seek?" They answered, "Rabbi, where are you staying?" (Jn 1:38). Jesus replied, "'Come and see.' They came and saw where he was staying; and they stayed with him that day, for it was about the tenth hour" (Jn 1:39).

One of these two men was Andrew. Since Andrew was Simon Peter's brother, knowing Andrew will give us a better understanding of what kind of man the first pope was. Andrew was on the cutting edge of religion; when he learned about John the Baptist, he went to John to be baptized, and then followed him as a disciple. And when the Baptist pointed out Jesus, Andrew immediately became a follower of Christ. After spending the day with Jesus, we are told that Andrew went looking for his brother Simon. Andrew was so excited that, as soon as he saw him, he blurted out, "We have found the Messiah" (Jn 1:41). These are the first words that Christ's chief Apostle ever heard about Jesus, and they are extremely profound. The Jews had been waiting for the Messiah for over five hundred years, and here comes Andrew saying, "We have found the Messiah." It's important to notice the very first thing Andrew does: He brings his brother to Jesus. What a beautiful gesture. Here, at the beginning of John's Gospel, we have the first example of evangelization.

At this point, Andrew doesn't have a deep understanding of Christology. In fact, he has only known Jesus for about twenty-four hours. But he knows that Jesus is the Messiah, and Andrew also knows his brother, so he introduces the two. This gets right to the heart of evangelization. As St. John Paul II told us, all you need is to know Jesus Christ and to know modern men and women with all of their insecurities, hopes, and fears, and introduce them to Jesus Christ. Sometimes we make things too complicated. We think that evangelization means to give someone the whole of Catholic Tradition, Scripture, and theology. In the end, we get so overwhelmed that we don't even begin. But if you've ever introduced two people who didn't know each other, you're already equipped. That is all evangelization is—introducing two people.

Now, Jesus had already heard about Simon. Andrew probably had talked about his older brother all day. So Jesus met him and said, "So you are Simon the son of John? You shall be called Ce'phas" (Jn 1:42). *Cephas* is an Aramaic word that means "rock." In Greek, the word is translated *petros*, and it is from this Greek translation that we get the name "Peter." We'll go over these names again in more detail in a later chapter.

The next day, Jesus decided they should go to Galilee, a short journey north along the River Jordan. There he encountered Philip, to whom he extended the simple invitation, "Follow me" (Jn 1:43). Philip was from Bethsaida, the same village as Andrew and Simon Peter. (From now on, we will refer to him mainly as "Peter.") Although Peter was living in Capernaum, his hometown was Bethsaida, so he would have known Philip. Notice the simple chain of evangelization: Andrew knows Simon Peter and introduces him to Christ. Andrew and Peter know Philip, and so introduce him to Christ. From the beginning, evangelization has been relational.

We see the friendship between Andrew and Philip later in the sixth chapter of John's Gospel, when Jesus, before multiplying the loaves and fishes to feed the multitude, turns to Philip and asks where they can buy food for the crowds. Of course, it wasn't possible to buy that much bread, so Philip is given the task of finding what is available. Philip turns to Andrew for help, and Andrew finds the boy with the five loaves and two fish.

Later, in the twelfth chapter of John's Gospel, we read that some Greeks had come to worship at the feast of Passover. They came to Philip and said, "Sir, we wish to see Jesus" (Jn 12:21). Philip then took their request to Andrew. Notice how you go down the chain and back—Andrew introduces Philip to Jesus, and now Philip goes to Andrew to get to Jesus.

Hellenistic Influence

Why did the Greeks single out Philip from among the Twelve when they came for Passover? It was most likely because he spoke Greek. Since both Philip and Andrew were from Bethsaida, which had a sizable Jewish and Gentile population, they were probably more open to Greeks coming to know Jesus. The Greeks may also have approached Philip because he had a Greek name, not a Jewish one. (Andrew and Simon had Greek names as well—Simon was the Greek form of the Jewish name Simeon.)

Before being conquered by the Romans, Israel had been ruled by Greeks, and we know that Bethsaida was Hellenistic in culture. At this time, however, the territory comprising ancient Israel was co-ruled—at the discretion of the Romans, of course—by two sons of the late Herod the Great. Each had his own dominion. The Apostle Philip had the same name as one of them, Philip the Tetrarch, brother of Herod Antipas. The region ruled by Philip was the Decapolis and the area around Bethsaida—the region east of the Sea of Galilee, into which the Jordan flows. On the west of the Jordan was the area of Galilee proper, where Herod Antipas ruled. In AD 30, Philip gave Bethsaida the title of *polis* (Greek, meaning "city") and made it the capital of his territory.

It is unknown why Peter and Andrew moved from their hometown of Bethsaida to Capernaum, which was only three miles away. Biblical scholars, however, have come up with different hypotheses since it was unusual for first-century Jews to move away from their hometowns. A plausible theory is that they moved after Philip the Tetrarch made Bethsaida his capital and dedicated a pagan temple there, naming it Julia in honor of the wife of Caesar Augustus. Having a pagan temple in their village would have been extremely offensive to Peter and Andrew, who were devout Jews. We know they were devout and observant Jews because Andrew was a disciple of John the Baptist, and Peter, when he had a vision of unclean animals, stated, "I have never eaten anything that is common or unclean" (Acts 10:14). Recent archaeological work around Bethsaida has unearthed many pig bones, which tells us that there were most likely Jews who compromised with the Hellenistic culture and ate pork and other unclean (or unkosher) foods. But Peter wasn't among them. You can imagine that faced with a pagan temple and Hellenistic culture, Peter and Andrew would have wanted to move to Capernaum, which was more pious and zealously Jewish.

It is also important to note that if you were from Bethsaida, you probably knew enough Greek to get by. This means that along with their Greek names, Simon Peter, Andrew, and Philip most probably spoke at least some Greek. The benefit of a Galilean fisherman knowing the Greek language and culture will become significant later on. For now, it is interesting to note that God, in his infinite wisdom, placed Peter in a Hellenistic-Jewish village that prepared him for God's plan. As we will see later, such seemingly insignificant details were actually quite important to prepare Peter for his great commission from Christ.

Peter's Call to Cast into the Deep

At this time, Peter the fisherman was still running the family business. His primary role was to support the family, and, in particular, his younger brother Andrew, who was a full time disciple of John the Baptist. This sets the scene for the encounter with Jesus, which we see in the fifth chapter of Luke's Gospel, when Jesus tells Peter to "*duc in altum*" ("cast into the deep").

Luke's Gospel tells us that "the people pressed upon him to hear the word of God" and that "he was standing by the lake of Gennesaret" (Lk 5:1). This particular lake also was called the Sea of Galilee and, officially, the Sea of Tiberias. (The local residents didn't like their lake being renamed after a Roman emperor, so Sea of Tiberias was not popular.) The name Gennesaret—meaning "harp," in reference to the shape of the lake—was the name preferred before the time of Christ. This had changed by the first century, however, when it became more common to refer to the lake as the Sea of Galilee. All three names are used in the Gospels.

When Christ approached the Sea of Galilee, he saw two boats by the lake. The fishermen, however, were already washing their nets. This indicates that it was early to mid-morning. Fisherman would work all night, as Simon Peter will tell us in a few minutes, and then return in the morning. Arriving on shore, they would unload their fish at Magdala, a processing place for salting and drying the fish to be sold in the markets. Afterwards, they would return to their boats and wash their nets.

Perhaps, as the family businessman, Peter was not as devout as his brother Andrew, who always liked to be at the feet of John the Baptist. So what does Jesus do? He takes his teaching right over to the boats on shore so that Peter can hear what he has to say. He sees that Peter's boat is empty, and so he gets in and tells Peter to pull out a little from the land. This tells us something about Jesus's character. He was not a mild-mannered man. He arrives and takes command.

This was a clever way to get Peter involved in the "Bible study." Sometimes when we evangelize, we have to come up with clever ways to attract people. In this case, Jesus sat right down in Peter's boat and began to teach the multitude. This makes even more sense when you consider that there are many little bays along the northern shore of the Sea of Galilee near Capernaum. In the days before microphones and loud speakers, the crowd had to press upon him to hear. But now, with his voice carrying over the water, the acoustics would have allowed the large crowd to hear him perfectly. Perhaps even more importantly, Peter is a captive audience. While he is manning the boat, he has no choice but to listen to Jesus.

"And when he had ceased speaking, he said to Simon, *'duc in altum'* (put out into the deep) and let down your nets for a catch" (Lk 5:4). It was in explaining these verses in a letter written in the Jubilee year (1999) that Pope St. John Paul II opened up what in some ways was his last will and testament. In this letter, which celebrating two thousand years of Catholic history, he was preparing the Church for the next thousand years—and he started everything off with *duc in altum*. He was telling us that while the last two thousand years were impressive, we can't be afraid of the future. Even in the midst of what seem to be insurmountable challenges, we can't be afraid of the future. To reinforce this, he quotes from the Epistle to the Hebrews: "Jesus Christ is the same yesterday and today and for ever" (Heb 13:8). The same God who has blessed the Church for the last two thousand years will continue to bless her.

When Christ says *duc in altum*, Peter replies, "Master." In Greek, this is translated as *epistata*, which denotes a title of respect. "Master, we toiled all night and took nothing!" (Lk 5:5). There is a slight pause, as if Peter is waiting for Jesus to say something. But Jesus says nothing, so Peter continues, "But at your word I will let down the nets" (Lk 5:5). Peter would obey, even when it didn't make sense—even when the prospects didn't look good. This was exactly what St. John Paul II was saying. *Duc in altum.* Go and evangelize the world, even when you think that the world is not ready— even when you think the world doesn't want you. Don't worry if you've toiled and failed. Failing to persevere is the only failure.

"And when they had done this, they enclosed a great shoal of fish; and as their nets were breaking, they beckoned to their partners in the other boat to come and help them. And they came and filled both the boats, so that they began to sink. But when Simon Peter saw it, he fell down at Jesus' knees, saying, 'Depart from me, for I am a sinful man, O Lord'" (Lk 6:6–8). The Greek term *kyrios*, which means "lord," indicates a change in Peter. Before, Peter had called Jesus "master." Now, he calls him the far loftier term, "Lord."

Andrew, the impetuous younger brother, understood right away that Jesus was the Messiah. Peter, the more seasoned, older brother, reserved his judgment. Jesus, however, had maneuvered the events perfectly—he got in Peter's boat, he spoke to Peter, and finally Peter witnessed Christ's actions. The word and then the deed. This is how Jesus moved Peter's heart to conversion.

Peter truthfully acknowledged that he was not worthy. Jesus responded, "Do not be afraid; henceforth you will be catching men" (Lk 5:10). Other translations have Jesus saying, "I will make you a fisher of men." Throughout the Old Testament, God is constantly telling Israel not to be afraid. Jesus was taking these words of God, "Do not be afraid," and speaking them to Peter. This is a great consolation for us, just as it was for Peter. Reflecting on Peter, the sinful and unworthy man, gives us great hope because we, too, are sinful and unworthy. But God doesn't call the worthy. He calls and, if we answer, makes us worthy—and tells us not to be afraid.

Chapter 2

Capernaum:
Village of Coming Consolation

In the last chapter, we saw how Jesus, Peter, and Andrew went to Galilee. But instead of going to Bethsaida, as you might expect since it was Peter and Andrew's hometown, they went to Capernaum, where Peter was living. In this chapter, we're going to focus on the village of Capernaum, and its importance in the Gospels.

Following the miraculous catch of fish, and the subsequent call of Peter, who would become a "fisher of men," we are told that they went back to the village of Capernaum where Jesus taught in the synagogue, and that afterwards they "entered the house of Simon and Andrew, with James and John" (Mk 1:29). This seemingly unimportant fishing village of about 1,500 people would become the headquarters of Jesus's public ministry in Galilee for the next three years. It's interesting to note how the relationship between Jesus and Peter developed. First, Jesus turned Peter's boat into his pulpit. Next, he moved into Peter's house. Jesus wanted Peter to be "all in."

Once in Capernaum, Jesus began working miracles of healing, even in Peter's own family. "Now Simon's mother-in-law lay sick with a fever, and immediately they told him of her. And he came and took her by the hand and lifted her up, and the fever left her" (Mk 1:30–31). What did Jesus do when he heard that Peter's mother-in-law was sick? He healed her. And we're told that she immediately got up and served them.

Later that evening, at sundown, the people of the village brought to Jesus all who were sickly as well as those possessed by demons. Mark's mention of the time of day, "sundown," is highly significant. For Jews, the Sabbath (*shavat* in Hebrew) is measured from sundown to sundown. The Pharisees—pious Jews of the time who strictly followed the Mosaic Law— taught that healing someone on the Sabbath broke the Law because it was a form of work, which the Sabbath forbade. It's interesting that Jesus healed Peter's mother-in-law on the Sabbath, but the other villagers waited until the Sabbath was over. At sundown, when the Sabbath had ended, everyone who needed healing rushed to Peter's house. We are told that Jesus healed many who were sick with various diseases and cast out many demons.

Following these miraculous healings and exorcisms, Jesus went to pray: "In the morning, a great while before day, he rose and went out to a lonely place, and there he prayed" (Mk 1:35). With Peter and Andrew, James and John, and Peter's mother-in-law all staying in the house, it was probably a little crowded. So Jesus got up early and went to find a quiet place to pray. What a powerful example of the importance of prayer.

Peter's Prominence in Mark's Gospel

The next verse tells us that "Simon and those who were with him followed him" (Mk 1:36). We'll see this phraseology, which gives Simon Peter prominence among the other disciples, again at the end of Mark's Gospel. This prominence of Peter in Mark's Gospel is further emphasized in the way that Christ first encountered his disciples. For example, John's Gospel tells us that Christ first encountered Andrew, who was at the River Jordan where John the Baptist was preaching, and that Andrew introduced Jesus to his brother. Mark, on the other hand, tells us that Christ encountered "Simon and Andrew" while they were fishing in the Sea of Galilee (*cf.* Mk 1:16). It's significant that, in Mark's Gospel, Simon Peter is the first of the disciples to be mentioned, and he's also the last one to be mentioned immediately after the Resurrection: When the women went to the tomb to anoint Christ's Body, the angels near the empty tomb told them to "go, tell his disciples and Peter that he is going before you to Galilee" (Mk 16:7). It's interesting that we see "Peter and the disciples" both at the very beginning and the very end of Mark's Gospel. In a sense, Peter brackets the beginning and ending of Mark's Gospel.

A common literary custom used by the Greeks when writing historical works was to tell the audience the identity of the primary eyewitness. This was done by bracketing their testimony with their name. Grammatically, we would call this an *inclusio*, which is a framing device. The fact that Peter is a bracket found at the beginning and end of Mark's Gospel tells us that Peter is the primary witness. For this reason, we can perhaps think of the Gospel of Mark as the "Gospel of Peter" as written by Mark.

This emphasis on Peter in Mark's Gospel becomes even more significant when we look at the person of Mark. According to Tradition, the Gospel of Mark was written by John Mark, who was a disciple of both the Apostle Paul and the Apostle Peter. Tradition also tells us that Mark accompanied Peter to Rome where he worked as his translator. Evidence of this can be found in the First Letter of Peter, where Peter sent greetings from himself and Mark, who is with him in "Babylon"—a code word for Rome. From this, we know that Mark was with Peter in Rome, and it also explains why Mark's Gospel has more Latin and contains more references to Roman culture than the other Gospels. For example, Mark uses the Roman system of dividing the night into four "watches."

Regarding the date of Mark's Gospel, St. Irenaeus (ca. AD 130–202) taught that, soon after the martyrdom of Peter, Mark wrote down Peter's teachings so they wouldn't be forgotten. For this reason, Mark's Gospel—as attested to by Papias of Hierapolis (ca. AD 70–163) and St. Irenaeus—has traditionally been considered to hold the apostolic witness of St. Peter. In any event, the earliest testimony that we have available tells us Mark's Gospel contains eyewitness testimony to the preaching of Peter.

Zebulun and Nephtali

Going back to the gospel story, we can ask why Jesus would choose Capernaum as his base of operations. At first glance, the obvious reason seems to be that Capernaum was where Peter lived. Christ went to Galilee to encounter Peter and Andrew, and it was a matter of convenience to stay in their home. However, there is a much deeper, prophetic reason that is carefully explained in Matthew's Gospel.

> Now when he heard that John had been arrested, he withdrew into Galilee; and leaving Nazareth he went and dwelt at Capernaum by the sea, in the territory of Zebulun and Nephtali. (Mt 4:12)

Each of the Twelve Tribes of Israel (except for the priestly tribe of Levi) was given a part of the Promised Land. The Tribes of Zebulun and Nephtali were given the northern region of the land, which included Capernaum where Peter was living. Matthew tells us that Jesus dwelt in Capernaum, "in the territory of Zebulun and Nephtali, that what was spoken by the prophet Isaiah might be fulfilled" (Mt 4:12–13). Christ's coming to Capernaum was to fulfill the oracle of Isaiah, which Matthew paraphrases by describing the region as "the land of Zebulun and the land of Nephtali, toward the sea, across the Jordan, Galilee of the Gentiles" (Mt 4:15, *cf.* Is 9:1–2).

This area was called "Galilee of the Gentiles" because it was the first part of the Promised Land to fall into Gentile hands. It fell to the Assyrians in 732 BC, which was a long time before Peter lived there. The Jews, however, have always been a very historical people, and they know their own history. You can almost hear a Jewish resident of Galilee at the time of Christ saying, "More than seven centuries ago, this land fell to the Assyrians, and that is why to this very day we call it 'Galilee of the Gentiles.'"

After the Jews were conquered by the Assyrians, it was not until the Maccabean period—when Judas Maccabeus and Simon Maccabeus defeated Antiochus Epiphanes and the Greek army—that Jews began to return from Babylon and resettle in the northern regions of Israel. In fact, we are told that Judas Maccabeus specifically wanted Jews to settle there so that they could lay claim to the Holy Land. Yet the resettlement of Galilee, which was begun by the Maccabees roughly five hundred years after it was conquered by the Assyrians, didn't really take hold until about sixty to seventy years before Jesus was born. Then, all of a sudden, in the generation before Jesus and Peter, things began to happen. There was a tremendous population growth around the Sea of Galilee, and new villages were settled and began to grow. The Jewish historian Josephus (ca. AD 37–100) describes this area of Galilee as very beautiful and also very populous in the first century AD.

Matthew, however, sees Galilee as the fulfillment of a prophecy. The point he is making is that under the Gentiles, darkness loomed over the land, but from this darkness the people of Zebulun and Nephtali would see a great light. This light was Christ. If you follow Matthew's Gospel you will see that a star—a great light—signifies the birth of the Messiah. Here, Matthew is telling us that the light has moved north from Bethlehem and is now shining over the territory of Zebulun and Nephtali. Matthew understands this as an important part of God's plan of salvation. The Tribes of Zebulun and Nephtali, which were the first part of the Davidic kingdom to be lost, would become the first to hear Christ, the New

David, preach about the new kingdom of God, which would begin exactly where the old kingdom began to decline. It's amazing how providential and truly fitting this reversal of fortune really is for Zebulun and Nephtali.

Capernaum, which is situated squarely between Zebulun and Nephtali, could not have been a better place for Christ to begin his public ministry. If you look at the map of the Sea of Galilee, you'll see that Capernaum is just a couple miles from the boundary between Zebulun and Nephtali. So, in a sense, Capernaum straddles the borderland between Zebulun and Nephtali.

The prophecy then tells us that "for those who sat in the region and shadow of death / light has dawned" (Mt 4:16). That is the context in which Jesus began to preach, saying, "Repent, for the kingdom of heaven is at hand" (Mt 4:17). He announced the new kingdom in exactly the same place where the old kingdom first fell into darkness.

Capernaum and the Promise of Consolation

In addition to the prophetic importance of Capernaum, there is also significance in the name Capernaum, which can be separated into two parts: *caper*, meaning "village," and *naum*, signifying "consolation." The Greek *Naum* (or *Naoum*) in Hebrew is *Nahum*, the name of one of the twelve minor prophets. So, Capernaum can literally mean the "village of Nahum" or the "village of consolation." It is the latter sense that matters most for us.

Ezekiel, Jeremiah, and Isaiah had all foretold that God would restore Israel and regather the Twelve Tribes. He would take his people from the four corners of the world, bring them back to their own land, and then restore the kingdom. It was for this reason that the Jews, who had been exiled in Babylon, decided to come back to these regions. When this particular village was resettled, the Jews decided to call it Capernaum—the village of consolation. Why consolation? Because consolation is the key word of the prophecy that marks the turning point of Israel in the Book of Isaiah (*cf.* 40:1). The first thirty-nine chapters of Isaiah are all about misfortune. Their collective message? That because Israel has violated the Mosaic Covenant and broken the Law, it will be sent into exile, face judgment, and be punished.

Israel's immediate prospects were awfully bleak, and if Isaiah had ended at Chapter 39, the people might have despaired. In Chapter 40, however, we are told that God ultimately will forgive the sins of Israel and restore the Israelites' fortunes. It begins with the message, "Comfort, comfort my people, says your God" (Is 40:1). Let Jerusalem know "that her warfare is ended, that her iniquity is pardoned, that she has received from the LORD's hand double for all her sins" (Is 40:2). God's promise that her sins are pardoned is the turning point of the story of Israel. Note that the first verse begins with the Hebrew word *nahum*, which is about consolation. Then the second verse tells us that sins will be forgiven. Jesus's words in the Beatitudes, "Blessed are those who mourn for they shall be comforted" (Mt 5:4), are taken from Isaiah 40:2. The people will be comforted because their sins are forgiven.

Finally, in the third verse, we hear about a "voice in the wilderness" whose purpose is to "prepare the way of the

Lord." The Lord is now returning to his people. This phrase played an important part in the preaching of John the Baptist. When the scribes and the Pharisees came to John and asked, "Who are you?" (Jn 1:19), they were really wanting to know if he was the promised Messiah. John the Baptist tells them, "I am not the Christ [Greek for Messiah].... I am the voice of one crying in the wilderness, 'Make straight the way of the Lord'" (Jn 1:20, 23).

The message of Isaiah is that the comfort and consolation, so deeply connected to the forgiveness of sins, will be ushered in by the return of the Lord to Israel. "Get you up to a high mountain, O Zion, herald of good tidings; lift up your voice with strength, O Jerusalem, herald of good tidings, lift it up, fear not; say to the cities of Judah, 'Behold your God!'" (Is 40:9). The oracle tells Zion (or Galilee in the New Testament) to cry out, "Behold your God!"

The episode in the Gospel of Luke, where Mary and Joseph take the baby Jesus to the Temple, illustrates the importance of this turning point in the story of Israel. When they arrived at the Temple, Mary and Joseph met an elderly man named Simeon, who was awaiting the *consolation* of Israel. What he was looking for could only be found in Isaiah 40:1. He knew the history of Israel for the past five hundred years, including its defeat by its enemies, its exile, and its many sufferings and humiliations—and he had personally witnessed the humiliation of Israel in recent history. He was waiting for Israel's fortunes to turn. He was waiting for the promises of Isaiah 40 to be fulfilled before he died. He was waiting for the Messiah.

In the Hebrew language, we would say that Simeon was waiting for *nahum*. But instead of *nahum*, Luke uses the Greek word *paraclesis*, and it is from *paraclesis* that we get the word "paraclete". This idea of *nahum* (consolation) was so important for the early Christians that they used that word to describe the Holy Spirit, the third Person of the Blessed Trinity—the Counselor, the Comforter, the Paraclete.

Going back to Simeon, Luke summarizes the entire hopes of Israel by pointing to this pious, elderly Jew who was awaiting the consolation (*paraclesis*) of Israel. And this consolation meant the forgiveness of sins. In fact, this forgiveness of sins is the catalyst for the restoration of Israel, and it marks the arrival of a new era. It is the age of the Messiah.

Consolation and the Forgiveness of Sins

As Christians we say that the Holy Spirit is the Comforter because he brings the forgiveness of sins. This relationship between the Holy Spirit and the forgiveness of sins is beautifully illustrated in John's Gospel, when, following the Resurrection, Christ appears in the Upper Room. He breathes on the Apostles and says, "Receive the Holy Spirit. If you forgive the sins of any, they are forgiven; if you retain the sins of any, they are retained" (Jn 20:22–23). The early Christians understood the forgiveness of sins and the Holy Spirit as naturally belonging together.

The Jews who returned from the Babylonian Exile at the end of the Maccabean era were likewise looking for the *nahum*, the *paraclesis*. They were looking for the consolation of Israel, and they were waiting for the Messiah. It is for this reason that this simple Jewish fishing village called Capernaum becomes the village of consolation (*nahum*). And it is for this reason that Jesus, immediately after leaving Nazareth, goes directly to the village of consolation.

It's curious to note that Mark's Gospel tells us that "when [Jesus] returned to Capernaum after some days, it was reported that he was at home" (Mk 2:1). Notice that Jesus was "at home," and home is Peter's house. At that time, "Many were gathered together, so that there was no longer room for them, not even about the door; and he was preaching the word to them. And they came, bringing to him a paralytic carried by four men" (Mk 2:2–3). This was the moment that the long awaited forgiveness of sins came to the village of *nahum*—to the village of consolation—for it was at this moment that Jesus announced the forgiveness of sins.

For Christians, we are used to hearing about forgiveness. In fact, it's so central to the Gospel that we get accustomed or almost immune to hearing about it. For us, Christ forgiving a man's sins seems natural and not at all an event of great importance. But it would have been very different for the Jews who heard those words for the first time. In the first thirty-nine chapters of Isaiah there is no forgiveness because Israel hasn't repented. It's not until the fortieth chapter that we hear the announcement of consolation and forgiveness. This is what the Jews were awaiting when Jesus announced the forgiveness of sins. He was announcing the arrival of the messianic age, the age of *nahum*, the age of consolation.

Consolation and God's New Thing

In October 2010, Pope Benedict XVI called for a synod on the New Evangelization, which would take place in October 2012. At the time, I was preparing to give a series of talks on the New Evangelization. Seeking discernment, I prayed, "Lord, what is the key to this New Evangelization?" One text came clearly to mind: Isaiah 43:18–19. The true significance of these verses became even more apparent a few months later at Sunday Mass. The Old Testament reading, which was from the forty-third chapter of Isaiah, was paired with the second chapter of Mark in the New Testament. The Church, in her wisdom, teaching, and guidance, has set Isaiah 43 as the backdrop to the story of the paralytic told in Mark's Gospel.

These verses from Isaiah begin, "Remember not the former things, nor consider the things of old. Behold, I am doing a new thing; now it springs forth, do you not perceive it? I will make a way in the wilderness and rivers in the desert" (Is 43:18–19). It's telling us not to focus on the past because God is doing a "new thing." The key to understanding the New Evangelization is the awareness that it's not about what we do; it's not about having the right program; in fact, it's not about *us* at all. The "new thing"—not only for the Jews in Jesus's time but also for us in the New Evangelization—is what God is doing. He is the main actor. We only need to be receptive to him and obedient to his will. This key idea of the New Evangelization should give us great hope. When we look ahead at the tremendous work that needs to be done and compare it to our lack of resources, our problems, and our challenges, it's easy to despair. The New Evangelization, though, is not about new programs that we are going to begin. It's about what God is going to do. God is the subject, the actor, and the protagonist of the New Evangelization. That, indeed, is good news!

When Isaiah tells us to forget the past because God is going to do a "new thing," we should remember the context in which this prophecy was made. The Davidic kingdom had been militarily, politically, and geographically defeated. The people had been conquered and exiled and the Temple destroyed. They were slaves in a foreign land. The people of Israel felt shame and guilt, and they knew that it was their own fault. They had broken the Law, violated the covenant, and rejected the prophets, and now they were being punished for their sins. You would expect them to be at the point of despair. There is a danger here that God's people—both in the Old Testament and today—can reduce their identity to being simply sinners and failures, instead of sons and daughters of God. Because of this, God has to tell them not to remember the former things. He is doing a "new thing." The good news is that every saint has a past and every sinner has a future. That's the lesson God is trying to teach his people. Why is God doing this? Because you are "the people whom I formed for myself" (Is 43:21).

Then, in verse twenty-five, we get the powerful line: "I am He who blots out your transgressions for my own sake, and I will not remember your sins" (Is 43:25). First, God promises to do a "new thing" for Israel, and then he tells them to forget their failures and their sinful past. Their past should not define their identity or become their prison. God is going to liberate them from their past and give them a new present and a new hope for the future. God doesn't stop there—he is also going to blot out their sins entirely. This applies especially to us. Not only should we forget the past, but God will also blot out our sins and remember them no more.

This teaching from Isaiah is beautifully illustrated by the story of a young Jesuit priest, Fr. Claude Colombiere, who in 1673 was sent to work in a parish. He was a little too zealous and a little too intellectual. Finally, the parishioners complained to his Jesuit superiors, who decided to move him to a convent, where he couldn't ruffle too many feathers. When he arrived there, the Mother Superior greeted him and told him that they were glad he came, but that they were having a little problem with a young novice who claimed that Jesus was appearing to her. This was problematic for the Mother Superior because it was disturbing the whole convent. It was especially disturbing because, in these visions, Jesus opened his chest and showed his Sacred Heart.

The priest told the Mother Superior not to worry and to have the young novice identify herself to him in the confessional. So, Sr. Margaret Mary Alacoque went to confession with Fr. Colombiere. "Father, I'm the one to whom Jesus is appearing," she said. Fr. Colombiere asked her how often Jesus appeared to her. After she answered, he requested, "Would you ask Jesus a question for me?" Sr. Margaret Mary agreed to do so. He then told her, "Ask Jesus what I confessed in my last confession."

As Catholics know, the seal of confession is inviolable. The priest had come from a distant village, and he was new in the convent. Nobody could possibly know what he confessed in his last confession. He thought that he had set the perfect trap. Two weeks later, Sr. Margaret Mary came back to confession, and Fr. Colombiere asked her, "What did Jesus say?" Sister looked a little uncomfortable, and then replied, "When I asked Jesus the question that you requested of me, he answered, 'I don't remember.'" Here Jesus's words echo those found in Isaiah: "I am He who blots out your transgressions . . . and I will not remember your sins" (Is 43:25).

The brilliant young Jesuit theologian wasn't expecting that, and it opened him up to truly discern what was going on. He came to believe that Sr. Margaret Mary was really seeing Jesus, and it transformed his life; that is, he became a saint. In fact, devotion to the Sacred Heart became widespread throughout the Catholic Church, and, years later, St. John Paul II canonized Fr. Colombiere and, of course, Sr. Margaret Mary Alacoque. At the core of this devotion to the Sacred Heart is the good news announced in Isaiah: "Remember not the former things, nor consider the things of old. Behold, I am doing a new thing" (Is 43:18).

The Paralytic Embraces God's New Thing

As we examine Christ's healing of the paralytic man, it helps to take a more detailed look at Peter's house where Jesus was teaching the gathered crowd. An ordinary first-century Jewish home would have been a little larger than what we might expect at first. Normally, there would have been a central courtyard and a common kitchen area surrounded by several different rooms. When a son got married, he usually didn't move out of his parents' home and build a new house for himself and his bride. Rather, the family would add on an extra room. You can see this feature—a courtyard surrounded by several different rooms—in the ruins of Capernaum today. In most of the archaeological excavations done in Capernaum, there is also evidence of staircases located in the courtyard that led up to thatched roofs. The purpose of these staircases was to allow easy access to the roof, where the family would have stored various items. Normally, the foundation of these staircases and the first few steps were made of stone, but after a few feet the steps changed to mud bricks, which were much lighter.

At this point in the gospel scene, Jesus was teaching inside the house in a room adjacent to the courtyard. Because of the large crowd, the men carrying the paralytic couldn't get close to Jesus, so they went up on the roof where they tore through the thatching to lower the paralytic down. Peter shows uncharacteristic restraint as he's watching them rip through his roof. Or perhaps Mark, out of kindness, carefully edited out Peter's true reaction. In any event, the paralytic was lowered down through the roof and there encountered Christ, who not only healed his body but forgave his sins.

What happened when Jesus said that the paralytic's sins were forgiven? The scribes and Pharisees began to murmur, "Why does this man speak thus? It is blasphemy! Who can forgive sins but God alone?" (Mk 2:7). They were thinking about the former things. They were thinking about the Temple sacrifices and the old ways of dealing with sin. But there was a "new thing" going on right in front of their eyes. There was a new Exodus, and they didn't see it because they were holding onto the old ways.

What moves me the most about this episode is what the paralytic did when Jesus told him, "Rise, take up your pallet and go home" (Mk 2:11). "He rose, and immediately took up the pallet and went out before them all" (Mk 2:11). Let's think about this. Jesus had just asked him to do the impossible—to stand up and walk—something that he clearly could not do. Jesus didn't act like a physician, examining the legs, rubbing them down or applying medicine, or even asking him what the symptoms were or if he had any feeling in his legs. No. Jesus simply gave him a command: Stand up. How easy it would have been for the paralytic to remember the former things. To remember the disability that had defined him for so many years. He could have replied, "I would like to rise, sir, but my legs just don't work." But instead, he put away the past and was open to the "new things" that God wanted to do in his heart and in his life. That changed everything.

So here we are in Peter's house, where Jesus announces the good news foretold by Isaiah about a new Exodus. "Remember not the former things, nor consider the things of old. Behold, I am doing a new thing" (Is 43:18). We need to reflect on this story to see how God wants to transform our hearts and our lives, and the lives of those around us. Oftentimes, we put people in categories. We'll say something like, "This person will never be open to God." We look at their past—or our own past—and think that things will never change. We get stuck in a mold, and we're not open to God's transforming grace. We need to turn to God and ask that he give us courage to open our eyes to the "new thing" that he wants us to do in this New Evangelization, the "new thing" that he wants us to do in the Church and in our hearts and in the lives of the people around us. We need to ask for courage and the foresight of the paralytic so that we, too, might rise and walk.

Chapter 3

Faith Not Fear: Walking in Trust

Having reflected on the prophetic meaning of the village of Capernaum in the last chapter, we'll now turn to a few stories, centered mostly around Peter and his boat, to help us better understand Peter. We'll look at four key scenes in the Gospel of Matthew and, in each of these, examine how Jesus spoke with the disciples and challenged them in their faith.

The key phrase that we will see repeated in each of these gospel scenes is the line: "O men of little faith" (Mt 6:30; 8:26; 14:31; 16:8). The word translated as "little," however, has a much stronger meaning in the original Greek. It might be better translated as "O men of *dinky* faith," since "dinky" really emphasizes the point of what Christ was trying to tell the Apostles. Christ used this type of language to challenge his disciples to trust wholeheartedly in God the Father. It's important to remember that this message was not just for these first disciples—it is also meant for us. If we are going to be his followers, we too have to be pushed and stretched so that our faith and trust in God can grow. One thing that is striking in these four episodes is the pattern that emerges. The first episode parallels the fourth, and the second parallels the third, forming a type of concentric cycle.

This repetition is an invitation to a kind of *lectio divina*—a spiritual reading of Scripture that leads us toward deeper meditation and reflection.

The Sermon on the Mount

The first of the four scenes is from the Sermon on the Mount (*cf.* Mt 6:30) when Jesus refers to God as "Father." Although calling God "Father" was not unheard of in the Old Testament, it was certainly not common; and so Jesus's language would have come across as somewhat strong to those listening to his words for the first time. As if to drive home the point, Jesus referred to God as Father not just once but seventeen times in the Sermon on the Mount.

Beginning with Matthew 6:30, Christ exhorts his listeners to trust in God's fatherly providence:

> "If God so clothes the grass of the field, which today is alive and tomorrow is thrown into the oven, will he not much more clothe you, O you of little faith? Therefore do not be anxious, saying, 'What shall we eat?' or 'What shall we drink?' or 'What shall we wear?' For the Gentiles seek all these things; and your heavenly Father knows that you need them all. But seek first his kingdom and his righteousness, and all these things shall be yours as well." (Mt 6:30–33)

Notice the priority that Jesus gave each of these statements. Seek *first* the kingdom of God, and *then* these other things will come to you. In other words, Christ was challenging his followers to do the opposite of the Gentiles, who sought comfort, security, and worldly things before giving any thought to the divine. He was telling them that God was their Father, and he knew all of their needs and would provide for them. When we trust in God's fatherly care and seek his will rather than our own, we become free of anxiety and fear.

I find it especially interesting that Jesus first spoke about freedom from anxiety in meeting their daily needs—clothing, food, and drink—and then, immediately afterwards, challenged them to store up treasure in Heaven. He was telling them that they couldn't serve both God and money. From a Jewish perspective, Jesus was speaking about the *gemilut hasadim*, which refers to works of mercy. He was basically asking them to be generous with what they had. People who don't have faith are often afraid to be generous because they look at the future, which is uncertain. When you see an uncertain future, you can't be sure what you can safely give away in the present because you don't know how much you are going to need later. It's always striking to me that when studies are done on generosity and giving, the results consistently show that people who aren't religious give less than one percent of their income to charitable causes. However, people who identify themselves as devout—regardless of whether they are Jewish, Catholic, or Protestant—give a much higher percentage. On a superficial level, you might say that religious people are just more caring or sensitive to the needs of others. However, I believe there is a much deeper reason behind this. People who are more "religious" have more faith in God as a good and loving Father who provides for his children. Because of this, they are freer to give generously of their goods without fearing what the future might bring.

The greatest obstacle to generosity is not the meanness and hardness of heart of people like Ebenezer Scrooge. Rather, the greatest impediment to generosity is fear of the future. And the opposite of fear is faith. So this was the challenge that Christ was giving his listeners. If you want to be a disciple of Christ, you can't live in fear of the future like the Gentiles. Rather, you must "seek first his kingdom and his righteousness, and all these things shall be yours as well" (Mt 6:33). When we put this in the context of the Sermon on the Mount, the larger meaning becomes even more profound. Jesus is teaching us to be a child of God and to trust in God as our heavenly Father. As Christ rhetorically asks, if God provides for the birds of the air and the flowers of the field, how much more will he provide for you?

A Storm on the Sea of Galilee

This teaching from the Sermon on the Mount leads us into the next scene, when Jesus again admonished the Apostles as men of little faith. In Matthew 8:23, we find Christ and his disciples out in a boat. "And when he got into the boat, his disciples followed him. And behold, there arose a great storm on the sea, so that the boat was being swamped by the waves" (Mt 8:23–24).

To put this in context, the Sea of Galilee experiences many large storms, which can come up suddenly, especially in the rainy season. To make matters worse, the sea is surrounded by mountains, which form large shells around the lake, making the wind constantly shift directions. These strong and unpredictable winds are precisely what put Peter's boat in jeopardy. In fact, it would have been even more treacherous for Peter, considering that most fishing boats used on the Sea of Galilee in the first century had flat bottoms that enabled them to reach the best fishing grounds located in the shallow waters on the northern shore, where warm water enters the lake from the River Jordan and various springs. Fishermen in Peter's time would have worked these waters especially in winter, when the tilapia could be found there in abundance. While the boat's flat bottoms helped the fishermen navigate shallow waters more expertly, they also made the boats less stable vessels that were easily whipped about by the winds and waves.

As the storm picked up strength, the boat began to take on water to the point that it was in serious danger of being swamped. The disciples were frightened and panicking, but Jesus remained fast asleep in the stern. "And they went and woke him, saying, 'Save us, Lord; we are perishing'" (Mt 8:25). You can sense the urgency and panic in these words. But how does Christ answer? "'Why are you afraid, O men of little faith?' Then he rose and rebuked the winds and the sea; and there was a great calm" (Mt 8:26).

Think about the tremendous magnitude of what Christ did here. Two of the least controllable forces in the world are the winds and waves. Modern technology can monitor them and, at best, predict them with only limited success. They represent the epitome of nature's power. Think of a hurricane. There is nothing that we can do to diminish its powerful winds or destructive waves. Yet, Jesus rose in the boat and rebuked the wind and the waves. And they obeyed. This is extraordinary. He masters nature in its rawest power and most uncontrollable form.

When Rembrandt was only twenty-nine years old, he painted this gospel scene in which Peter's boat was being thrashed about by the wind and the waves. His point was to show us that a storm can be waiting at any moment. But more importantly, it shows us the proper response to the storm. It's interesting to note how many people are in the boat. Most people glance at the painting quickly and answer thirteen—Jesus plus the Twelve Apostles. However, if you count the figures carefully, there are fourteen. Rembrandt painted himself into the scene. This reflects the ancient practice of *lectio divina*—the practice of putting ourselves in the biblical scene, asking: What would it be like if I were there? What would I be doing? What would I see? What would I hear? What would I feel? This practice of putting ourselves in the scene is part of the genius of St. Ignatius of Loyola and the reflections in his *Spiritual Exercises*.

In the painting, there are three groups of disciples. In the back of the boat, there's a small group who, in the midst of the storm, is gathered at Jesus's feet and keep their eyes focused on him. There is a great calm surrounding this group. In fact, the painting shows a light coming from Christ, and those gathered around Christ share in that light. In great contrast to this light, there is darkness on the other end of the boat. And where this darkness reigns, a second group of disciples is hidden in the shadows. There is a tremendous message in the way Rembrandt uses light in this painting. There is the humble light of Christ that shines in the midst of the darkness, and the Apostles who keep their eyes on Christ share in his light and possess a sense of calm. In contrast, those who do not have their eyes fixed on Christ are greatly disturbed by the wind and the waves and are possessed by the fear and darkness.

Storm on Sea of Galilee by Rembrandt

There is also a third group of disciples, probably seasoned fisherman, fighting the storm and desperately trying to keep the boat from being swamped. And in the midst of this group we see Peter fighting the storm with everything he's got. We often identify with Peter, trying to take control of our lives and all of the problems that arise. We assume that if we just work harder, then we can make this or that happen. This reliance on our own efforts makes us sort of a Pelagian Peter. Pelagianism was a fourth-century heresy that taught that man was not tainted by Original Sin and that we could choose to do good and, therefore, achieve salvation without the grace of God.

Rembrandt also depicts a light coming through the clouds, which indicates that the storm is about to break. The irony is that Peter has his back to this light. This often happens in the storms that arise in our lives. When we fight the storms on our own, we are oblivious to the light. We see only darkness. We don't see the hope, only the despair. We're not focused on the future, but only on the present problem. When we feel this way, I find that it's good to dwell on the Apostle John. He's there in the back with Jesus, looking to the light and relying on Jesus to get the boat through the storm.

In the midst of this great storm, Christ again says to his Apostles, "Why are you afraid, O men of little faith?" (Mt 8:26). And then, after he commanded the storm to subside and a great calm overtook the Sea of Galilee, "The men marveled, saying, 'What sort of man is this, that even winds and sea obey him?'" (Mt 8:27). Something incredible had happened.

Jesus Walks on the Water

The next episode in Matthew's Gospel that helps us to understand Peter is in the fourteenth chapter, following the multiplication of the loaves and fishes. Jesus asked the disciples to get into the boat and go before him to the other side of the lake. Then he dismissed the crowds and went up to the hills by himself to pray; and, when evening came, he was there alone. By this time, the boat was a furlong's distance from land. The problem was that Jesus told the disciples to take the boat and go to the other side of the lake, and that he would catch up with them. But how? The sixth chapter of John highlights the fact that there was no boat for Jesus.

Matthew tells us that during the fourth watch of the night another storm came up, and the wind was against them. At that moment, the Apostles saw Christ coming toward them, walking on the sea. When they saw this, they were terrified and cried out, "It is a ghost!" (Mt 14:26). Here, you have these seasoned fisherman—all strong, tough men—crying out in fear because they think they've seen an apparition, phantom, or demon coming out of the midst of the storm to get them. They were in a state of utter panic, but immediately Jesus spoke to them saying, "Take heart, it is I; have no fear" (Mt 14:27). There are three parts to these words of Christ. The first is to take heart; the second is when Christ identifies himself; and the third is when he tells them not to be afraid.

What is it that will cause them to take heart? It is Christ himself. The Greek words by which Christ identifies himself in Matthew's Gospel are *ego eimi*. Many Bibles translate these words as "it is I," which really doesn't capture the meaning of the Greek. In the Septuagint translation of Exodus 3:14, when God asks Moses for his name, God replies *ego eimi* ("I AM WHO I AM"). In Hebrew, this is rendered *Ehyeh Asher Ehyeh*.

In this instance, we have Jesus walking on the water, and the Apostles believing they have seen a ghost. Christ doesn't just respond, "Don't worry, it's me." Using the Old Testament formula he says, "I AM." This episode brings to mind Job 9:8, which speaks about him who "trampled the waves of the sea." Job is telling us that God alone can walk on the waters, and here we have Christ doing exactly that and using the divine name "I AM." Literally translated, this verse tells us, "Take heart, I AM; have no fear."

"And Peter answered him, 'Lord, if it is you, bid me come to you on the water'" (Mt 14:28). Peter had spent his whole life on the Sea of Galilee. Seeing Jesus walk on the water, he marveled—and wanted to do the same. This spontaneous reaction of Peter reminds us of the time when Jesus told his disciples that unless they became like little children, they could not enter the kingdom of Heaven. When children see something they like, the first thing they want to know is if they can do it, too. Here we see the childlike nature of Peter in its fullness.

Curiously, you don't get this reaction from the other Apostles. Peter was the only one to ask if he could walk on the water. God loves boldness—and childlike trust and abandonment. When we abandon ourselves to God, he will come through and catch us every time. He wants us to radically trust in him. Unfortunately, instead of acting like children who completely trust in their parents, we usually start thinking like adults. We play it safe and careful, and we don't step out in trust and give God the opportunity to do great things in our lives, in the Church, and in the world.

In a tremendous act of childlike faith, Peter got out of the boat and walked on the water. Everything was going well, but then he started to pay attention to the wind and the waves, and he was afraid. Fear is the enemy of faith. Fear crowds out faith like weeds choke flowers. If we want to live by faith, we have to uproot our fears and anxieties. It takes work, but we have to do this if we want to cultivate a vibrant and living faith. Why did Peter sink? He took his eyes off Christ and started to focus on the wind and the waves. The same holds true for us. Every time we take our eyes off Christ and start focusing on the problems and obstacles that we face, we start to sink. We must focus on the good news of Jesus Christ and not on the bad news that the world has to offer.

As Peter began to sink, he cried out, "Lord, save me" (Mt 14:30). This is the great Petrine prayer. I would encourage you to memorize this prayer, to meditate on it, and to truly pray it. Write it down so that you can pull it out of your pocket any time: "Lord, save me." It works. Peter got right to the point. He was afraid, so he cried to the Lord for help. Then what happened? Jesus reached out and caught him, saying, "O you of little faith, why did you doubt?" (Mt 14:31). Here's the extraordinary thing. Peter was the one who exhibited a true childlike faith, who actually got out of the boat and walked on water, yet he was the one who was told that he had a "dinky" faith. What does that make the other eleven who were too frightened to even try? Remember that Christ speaks to us just as he spoke to Peter.

When we get distracted from our mission, he says to us, "O man or woman of little faith, why did you doubt?" He calls us to realign our vision on him. The episode ends by telling us that when they got into the boat, the wind ceased. "And those in the boat worshiped him, saying, 'Truly you are the Son of God'" (Mt 14:33).

In 1994, St. John Paul II wrote a worldwide best seller entitled *Crossing the Threshold of Hope*. Although the Church had been going through some especially difficult times, his book didn't focus on the problems. Rather, he spoke about a "new springtime" for the Church, which illustrated his belief that the Church was coming out of its long winter. Over the previous decades, many people became discouraged by inclement ecclesial weather, but St. John Paul II never did. He kept looking for the light and the hope. Psalm 130, known in Latin as *De profundis*, says, "My soul waits for the LORD more than watchmen for the morning" (v. 6). In 1999, George Weigel wrote his biography of St. John Paul II—another best seller. He ended it by relating how the long-reigning pontiff would often get up early in the morning to watch the sun rise. St. John Paul II loved and often quoted these words: "My soul waits for the LORD more than watchmen for the morning." St. John Paul II was a watchman waiting for the light.

Going back to Rembrandt's painting, recall that Peter didn't see the light. Rather, he only focused on the storm and panicked, crying out on behalf of the Apostles, "Save us, Lord, we are perishing." Christ replied, "O men of little faith." Later, Peter walked on the water but again took his eyes off Christ and began to sink. Once more, Christ replied, "O man of little faith."

A Lack of Bread on the Sea of Galilee

The fourth time that we encounter the phrase "O men of little faith" is in Matthew 16:8, which will be the catalyst for the next chapter. The Apostles were traveling in a boat to the other side of the lake (v. 5), but they had forgotten to bring bread, and Jesus admonished them about the leavening of the Pharisees and of Herod. Because they misunderstood what he meant—we will examine what he meant in the next chapter—they remained anxious about having no bread. In other words, they were worried about what they were going to eat. Using the now familiar phrase, Jesus admonished them, "O men of little faith." Then he asked, "Do you not remember the five loaves of the five thousand, and how many baskets you gathered? Or the seven loaves of the four thousand, and how many baskets you gathered?" (Mt 16:9–10).

These words take us back to the first episode that we examined from the Sermon on the Mount (*cf.* Mt 6:25–26), when Jesus told his disciples not to be concerned about necessities like food as God the Father always provides for them. Yet, here we are, a few chapters later, and the disciples have begun to worry about their material needs.

The Barque of Peter

These failings of the disciples should give us encouragement. Just as Peter was in the middle of the boat fighting the storm, we're in the middle of the world with all of its problems. Just as the Apostles were concerned about what they were to eat, we're often concerned with worldly affairs to the neglect of God and his plans. What Jesus is telling us is that when we embark on our mission—his mission—we can't lose our focus or take our eyes off the kingdom. We are in Peter's barque, which is the Church. We may be taking on water, and we may be struggling—whether due to attacks or persecutions or even scandals within—but we can't panic. We need to put our trust in Jesus and know that he is going to pilot the ship and calm the storm. No matter how dire the circumstances may seem, he will bring his Church safely into port. This is a powerful message about how we should live in the world and how we should live in the Church.

It's interesting that the Latin word for "boat" is *navis*, from which we get the English words "navigation," "navy," and "nave," which refers to the main body of a church. If you look at the ceiling in an old Roman basilica, the ribbing looks like the inside of an upside-down boat, and for this reason Christian Tradition has called it the nave. This symbolism reinforces the idea that the Church is the barque of Peter. It may be tossed about by the wind and the waves, but Christ won't let it get swamped.

Remember that St. John Paul II encouraged us to *duc in altum* ("cast into the deep"). We find the same message here in Matthew—we need to step out of our comfort zone and trust in God. The question that we should always be asking ourselves is whether we've become too comfortable in our discipleship. Are we trusting God the Father to provide for our needs? Are we walking on water toward Christ? When we fail, as we often do, we should ask God to increase our "dinky" faith and to teach us to trust wholeheartedly in him—to give us the courage to step out like Peter and to be childlike in our trust of our Father in Heaven.

Chapter 4

Peter the Rock:
The Primacy of Jesus

In the last chapter, we looked at four scenes in which Christ admonished his disciples as "men of little [dinky] faith." We begin this chapter by examining the fourth of these scenes in more detail. This is particularly important because it leads us directly into the sixteenth chapter of Matthew's Gospel, which marks the high water mark of Peter's life: when he is given the keys of the kingdom.

The Leaven of the Pharisees and Sadducees

"When the disciples reached the other side, they had forgotten to bring any bread" (Mt 16:5). Jesus warned them to "beware of the leaven of the Pharisees and the leaven of Herod" (Mk 8:15). The disciples, however, did not understand Jesus's reference to leaven and thought he was admonishing them because they forgot to bring food for their journey. In fact, this mention of leaven had a much deeper meaning. Leaven was a common metaphor in Jewish culture that had its origin in the Passover story. It represented corruption as well as human pride, arrogance, and egotism. These are traits that lead us to want to do things our way rather than God's way.

We see this metaphor in Paul's First Letter to the Corinthians when he says, "Cleanse out the old leaven that you may be new dough, as you really are unleavened. For Christ, our Paschal Lamb, has been sacrificed. Let us, therefore, celebrate the festival, not with the old leaven, the leaven of malice and evil, but with the unleavened bread of sincerity and truth" (1 Cor 5:7–8). Paul goes on to tell them not to be "puffed up," which is exactly what leaven does to bread. In the case of Herod the Tetrarch, leaven stood for pride, which was manifested by his desire to rebuild the kingdom of his father, Herod the Great. In the case of the Pharisees, leaven indicated their desire to make a great show of their piety.

Christ was telling the disciples that they should not be proud or puffed up. Remember, Jesus had just worked an incredible miracle, multiplying the loaves and fishes to feed a great multitude. From a worldly perspective, his ministry had become a great success. The Apostles, who were the closest followers of Jesus, had helped distribute the loaves and fishes and shared in his popularity. It would have been understandable for Peter and the other disciples to feel proud and puffed up, susceptible to thinking they were going to become very important people in the new kingdom that Christ was going to establish. Unfortunately, a couple of chapters later, we will see them arguing among themselves as to who is the greatest.

It is incredible that after thousands of people had witnessed the miraculous multiplication of the loaves and fishes, we read that the Pharisees and Sadducees came and asked Jesus to show them a sign, like Moses, to prove that he was a prophet or the Messiah. Responding with rough words, Jesus tells them that no sign will be given to their "evil and adulterous generation" except the "sign of Jonah" (Mt 16:4). At this point, Jesus doesn't explain this reference to the "sign of Jonah," but it will become important a few verses later. After telling the Pharisees and Sadducees that he would provide them no sign, Jesus turned to his disciples and warned them about the leaven of the Pharisees and Sadducees (or the leaven of Herod in Mark's Gospel). This is the backdrop of this fourth scene.

Jesus, the One Loaf

In Mark's Gospel, we are told, "Now they had forgotten to bring bread; and they had only one loaf with them in the boat" (Mk 8:14). This was not just any bread they had forgotten to bring. Jesus had just multiplied the seven loaves to feed four thousand people, and there were seven baskets left over (*cf.* Mk 8:1–10, Mt 15:32–39). The bread they had forgotten to bring was this bread of the miracle. Because the disciples didn't understand Christ's warning against the "leaven of the Pharisees and the leaven of Herod," they began discussing its meaning among themselves. Earlier, when we first saw the phrase "O men of little faith" in the Sermon on the Mount, Jesus had told his disciples to not be anxious about what they were to eat and drink. At this moment, unfortunately, the disciples were doing just that—discussing the fact that they had no bread to eat. Aware of their conversation, Jesus told them, "O men of little faith, why do you discuss among yourselves the fact that you have no bread?" (Mt 16:8).

There's an irony in their discussion about having no bread. As we were told earlier, they actually had "one loaf" (*cf.* Mk 8:14). Why, then, were they discussing the fact that they had "no bread"? It is because Jesus is the bread of life. He is the "one loaf" mentioned in Mark's Gospel. They forgot the seven baskets of "miracle bread" left over and discussed the fact that they didn't have bread, failing to see that they had Christ—the one loaf—in the boat with them. This is why Christ asked, "Do you not yet perceive or understand?" (Mk 8:17). This comment is taken from Isaiah 43:19: "Behold, I am doing a new thing; now it springs forth, do you not perceive it?" Here again is a reference to this "new thing" that God is doing in their midst.

The reason they didn't perceive or understand can be found in Christ's next question: "Are your hearts hardened?" (Mk 8:17). This is an image from the Book of Exodus, which tells us that Pharaoh was so obstinate in refusing to free the Israelites from bondage—despite the pleading of Moses and Aaron, despite the miracles Moses performed before him, and despite the plagues that God visited upon Egypt until the last one convinced him it wasn't worth keeping the Israelites around—because he suffered a sort of spiritual blindness: namely, hardness of heart. Christ continued:

> "Having eyes do you not see, and having ears do you not hear? And do you not remember? When I broke the five loaves for the five thousand, how many baskets full of broken pieces did you take up?" They said to him, "Twelve." "And the seven for the four thousand, how many baskets full of broken pieces did you take up?" And

they said to him, "Seven." And he said to them, "Do you not yet understand?" (Mk 8:18–21)

The key here is the last question, "Do you not yet understand?" Understanding concerns the heart. Scripture often speaks about being blind or deaf to describe a person whose heart is hardened. Therefore, to understand about "this bread," i.e., to understand that Jesus is the bread of life, it takes a heart filled with faith. Not to understand the reference to bread means not to understand Jesus himself. That is the real point of the story.

The Blind Man in Bethsaida

As they were having this discussion about the bread, their boat pulled up to the dock in Bethsaida, the former hometown of Peter, Andrew, and Philip. In an earlier chapter, we discussed that they might have left Bethsaida because Philip the Tetrarch, the brother of Herod Antipas, had converted Bethsaida into his capital city and introduced a pagan culture that was offensive to the Jews. There was an intense rivalry between Herod and Philip, with each brother trying to outdo the other one. Herod stole Philip's wife Herodias and made his capital in a city on the Sea of Galilee, which he named Tiberias in honor of the Roman emperor. In return, Philip made his capital in Bethsaida, also on the Sea of Galilee.

As they came up to the docks, a blind man came to greet Jesus, who took the blind man by the hand and led him through the village, and then out of the village, away from the crowds. Once they were alone, Jesus spit in the mud and placed it on the man's eyes. The man saw, but his vision was not yet perfect. When Jesus asked how things appeared, the man answered, "I see men; but they look like trees, walking" (Mk 8:24). Why didn't the miracle work? At first glance, we might be tempted to say it was the blind man's fault. Perhaps he lacked faith. But it wasn't his fault. Jesus never upbraided him. He simply touched his eyes again and the man could see perfectly. Jesus healed the blind man in two stages just as he would Peter and the Apostles later.

Notice that Jesus took the blind man outside of the city before healing him, and after healing him, told the blind man not to go back to the city, saying, "Do not even enter the village" (Mk 8:26). It would have been much more convenient for Jesus to heal the man at the docks where he encountered him. Yet, Jesus led him all the way through the city to the other side, and then told him not to go back. Why? There was something about the city that the man needed to let go of in order to be healed and see clearly—to see Christ clearly. As the Beatitudes tell us, "Blessed are the pure in heart, for they shall see God" (Mt 5:8). Perhaps the blind man had to let go of the same thing that caused Peter, Andrew, and Philip to leave the city. Remember that Bethsaida was a place of pagan worship and culture. Jesus had to take the man out of this context so that he could see clearly. In a similar fashion, we can become blind to Christ and the ways of God if we put ourselves in a bad environment. The real question for us, then, is what is our Bethsaida? What is the place in our lives that Jesus wants to lead us away from because it has become a barrier to our relationship with God? Do we need to avoid something that has become an occasion of sin for us or causes spiritual blindness?

The Son of the Living God

After leaving Bethsaida, Jesus and his disciples traveled north toward the source of the River Jordan. It was while on this journey that Jesus asked them about his fundamental origin. "And Jesus went on with his disciples, to the villages of Caesare'a Philip'pi; and on the way he asked his disciples, 'Who do men say that I am?'" (Mk 8:27). He got a variety of answers, including one of the prophets, the prophet Elijah specifically, and John the Baptist come back from the dead. Jesus then turned and asked, "But who do you say that I am?" (Mk 8:29). He knew what the crowds were saying, but he wanted to know what the disciples believed. This was the fundamental question for the disciples, and it's still the fundamental question for us today. When we answer the question of who Jesus truly is, we're really answering the question of who we are as his disciples. If Jesus is the Christ, the Son of the living God, then that will define us and shape our lives. It will impact who we are and who we are called to be.

Peter characteristically jumped in and answered first, "You are the Christ, the Son of the living God" (Mt 16:16). This is Peter's great profession of faith—the key verse that contains the key teaching of this chapter. Peter is giving us a revelation. In return, Jesus responded:

"Blessed are you, Simon Bar-Jona! For flesh and blood has not revealed this to you, but my Father who is in heaven. And I tell you, you are Peter, and on this rock I will build my Church, and the gates of Hades shall not prevail against it. I will give you the keys of the kingdom of heaven, and whatever you bind on earth shall be bound in heaven, and whatever you loose on earth shall be loosed in heaven." (Mt 16:17–19)

Notice the exchanges in this dialogue between Jesus and Peter. First, Peter said that Jesus was the Christ or Messiah, the Son of the living God; then Jesus, in turn, told Peter that he was the "rock" upon whom he would build his Church. There is mutual revelation and mutual disclosure. Peter disclosed something profound about the identity of Christ, and Christ disclosed something profound about the identity of Peter. This new identity of Peter would reach even to his very name, which would be changed to "rock." It would also reach into his activity, which would be to bind and loose with the keys of the kingdom. Both Peter's identity and his activity would be reshaped by this encounter with Christ. But it all began with Peter making a profession of faith and a revelation about Jesus.

Often, we focus so much on the significance of what Jesus said to Peter, and the Petrine authority and papacy that flow from this, that we miss the importance of Peter's words. Jesus is the main actor in the story and we can learn a lot about him from this interaction. To fully understand Peter's words, "You are the Christ," we need to look at the meaning of the word *christ*, which is derived from the Greek translation of the Hebrew word *mashiah* (messiah in English). Both *christ* and *messiah* mean "anointed one." In the Old Testament, kings were anointed at their inauguration ceremonies. For example, we see in the tenth chapter of First Samuel that Saul was anointed with oil. Later, in the sixteenth chapter of First Samuel, David was anointed with oil as an indication that he had been chosen by God to replace Saul as king. Thus, the word *messiah* was another way of indicating kingship. Peter was basically saying that Jesus is the king, the heir of David foretold by the prophets and for whom all of Israel had been waiting. But even more than a king, he is the Son of the living God.

The fact that this dialogue took place at Caesarea Philippi also has tremendous significance. Overlooking the city was a large cliff with a cave or grotto down below. Immediately in front of the grotto was a pagan temple, which had been built by Herod the Great. The reason for building a temple in a city named after Caesar Augustus was entirely political. Following the assassination of his great uncle Julius Caesar in 44 BC, Octavian—later known as Caesar Augustus—sought vengeance on Julius's murderers, who included Brutus, Cassius, and some of the Roman senators. He went to the Roman senate and asked that they declare Julius a god. Some of the senators were rather cynical and didn't believe Julius was really a god—in fact, many believed he was a cruel tyrant who deserved his fate—but with Julius dead it was politically disadvantageous to oppose the declaration. Thinking that the now-deceased Julius could do them no harm, they went ahead and passed the declaration.

In a clever political maneuver, Octavian promptly declared himself the *divi filius* ("Son of God"). After all, Julius's will had named Octavian his adopted son and heir. Next, Octavian give himself the title "Augustus," or *Sebastia* in Greek, meaning "worthy of worship." And to the coins bearing his likeness, "Caesar Augustus" added the title of *divi filius*.

Temples soon began to be erected, especially in Asia Minor, or modern-day Turkey, to honor Caesar Augustus and to worship him as a god. Following suit, Herod the Great built three temples dedicated to Caesar Augustus, but he had to be very careful about their location. He couldn't build one in Jerusalem or there would have been a rebellion by the Jews. So he built one way up north in a city that was going to be named after Caesar. As the city was in the territory of Philip the Tetrarch, it was called Caesarea Philippi. Herod built another temple containing a large statue of Caesar Augustus in a seaport on Israel's northern coast, which he called Caesarea Maritima. That city would become the key port linking Israel with the rest of the Roman Empire, and it would be the port from which both Peter and Paul set sail for Rome. Herod built a third temple in the capital of Samaria, which he called Sebastia, the Greek word for Augustus.

Why would Herod build three temples dedicated to Caesar Augustus? In the civil war fought between Caesar Augustus, who controlled the western part of the Roman Empire, and Mark Antony, who controlled the eastern part, Herod had supported Antony. When Antony was defeated in the Battle of Actium in 31 BC and committed suicide, Herod was put in a precarious position. To save his throne, and perhaps his life, Herod wrote Caesar Augustus, apologizing and promising that he would be just as faithful to him as he had been to Mark Antony. As evidence of his loyalty, he built three temples in honor of Caesar Augustus.

It was at this precise moment, when Jesus and his disciples were standing in the city dominated by the temple dedicated to Caesar Augustus, who claimed to be the *divi filius*, the son of god, that Jesus asked the key question: "Who do you say that I am?" In essence, he was asking them to choose. Who is the true king? Who is the true Son of God? And it was here that Peter made his profession of faith: "You are the Christ, the Son of the living God" (Mt 16:16).

In the Old Testament, when the word "living" was used as a modifier for God, it was always in the context of contrasting the living God of Israel with the pagan idols of their Gentile neighbors. Statues of pagan gods were made of stone or silver or gold. They might have had a mouth, and ears, and eyes but they couldn't speak, or hear, or see. By saying Jesus was the son of the *living* God, Peter meant that he was more than a son of a politically-contrived god, as was Caesar Augustus. Rather, he was professing that Jesus is the Son of the living God—the true Son of the one true God. This would be *the* question for Peter for the rest of his life and for Christians over the next three centuries as they were told to burn incense to the image of the emperor and worship him or die. Over and over again, Christians would choose to be martyred because they followed in the footsteps of Peter by professing that there is only one living God—and it most certainly was not some Roman emperor.

A New Name, a New Mission

In response to Peter's profession, Jesus says, "Blessed are you." Blessings are extremely important in the Jewish tradition, and so Jesus begins by giving Peter a *barakah* ("blessing"). Note, he doesn't just say, "Well done, Peter, you're correct." He gives Peter a blessing: "Blessed are you Simon Bar-Jona!" (Mt 16:17). The word *bar* is Aramaic for "son," and the use of an Aramaic word in the middle of a Greek sentence makes it unique. Most likely, this Aramaic word was employed because this phrase is so idiomatic to the Old Testament that Matthew decided to preserve it in his Gospel. The name Bar-Jonah ("son of Jonah") is especially interesting because we know that the name of Peter's father was not Jonah but rather John. Remember from the first chapter when Jesus saw Peter and said, "So you are Simon the son of John?" (Jn 1:42). Later, in John 21, Jesus asks Peter three times, "Simon, son of John, do you love me?" Even more curious is the fact that Jonah was an extraordinarily rare name for a Jew in the first century. In fact, there is only one occurrence of this name in all of the Talmud, a central text of Rabbinic Judaism, and it refers to a woman. However, the name Jonah did occur a few verses earlier in the sixteenth chapter of Matthew. When the Pharisees and Sadducees asked for a sign, Christ told them that no sign would be given except for the "sign of Jonah." Here, Jesus changed Peter's surname to Bar-Jonah.

There is an important connection between Christ and Jonah, which comes from the Book of Jonah. Just as Jonah was in the belly of a great fish for three days and three nights,

Jesus would be in the tomb for three days and three nights. For this reason, one of Jesus's titles is the "New Jonah." However, notice the subtlety of the small details here. Jesus didn't change Peter's surname to Jonah, but rather Bar-Jonah. He was saying that Peter was now the son of Jonah—the son of the *New* Jonah, i.e., Jesus. He would be in the spiritual lineage of the New Jonah. Much more was going on here than a simple name change. Jesus was calling Peter to a profound and total transformation.

The second part of the name change concerns Peter's first name: "You are Peter, and on this rock I will build my Church" (Mt 16:18). If we insert the Greek words here, it would read, "You are *Petros*, and on this *petra* I will build my Church." The Greek word for "rock" is *petra*. Why then did Jesus call Peter *Petros* instead of *Petra*? The reason is that in the Greek language, *petros* is the masculine form of the word, while *petra* is the feminine form. When signifying "rock," the feminine form *petra* was used. When used as Peter's name, however, *petra* (rock) had to be changed to its masculine form *petros*. With this complete change of name, Peter, formerly known as "Simon, son of John," would thereafter be known as "Peter, son of Jonah."

Some non-Catholics, wanting to avoid the implications of this verse—particularly the Petrine ministry and the modern-day papacy—will argue that the word *petros* means "little rock" in Greek. Thus, by changing Simon's name to *Petros*, they contend that Christ actually was diminishing the role of Peter in the Church while emphasizing the *petra* ("big rock"), which referred to Christ himself or perhaps Peter's profession of faith. Yet, even if this was a reference to a small rock, the Bible frequently tells us about the great things a "little rock" can do. For example, in the Book of Daniel (*cf.* 2:35), Nebuchadnezzar made a statue of himself and wanted everyone to worship it. Yet a small stone shatters the statue and grows until it covers the world. This "stone" represents nothing less than Mt. Zion—in other words, the belief that the one true God will cover the whole world and shatter the pagan idols. In a sense, it doesn't matter whether Peter is a big or small rock because God is building on a foundation that will start out small but which is destined to cover the face of the earth, i.e., it is destined to be catholic or universal.

It's also important to remember that Jesus would not have been speaking to his disciples in Greek but rather in their native tongue, which was Aramaic. In Aramaic the word meaning "rock" was *cephas*, which does not have a masculine or feminine form. Thus, in Aramaic, Jesus's statement would be rendered, "You are *Cephas* (rock), and on this *cephas* (rock) I will build my Church." The size of the rock meant nothing in the original dialogue between Jesus and Peter.

In Scripture, a name change always signifies that a person is being given a new mission. For example, in the Book of Genesis, we see that Abram's name, which means "exalted father," was changed to Abraham, which means "father of many nations" (Gn 17:5). This name change indicated his new mission as the patriarch of the Jewish people. The name change also comes with a covenant—the Abrahamic covenant. Later in Genesis, we have the example of Abraham's grandson Jacob, whose name was changed to Israel. As was the case with Abraham, this change transformed Jacob's entire identity. He would become the patriarch not only of twelve sons but of the Twelve Tribes of Israel.

Another example of the significance of a name change, especially as it applies to "rock," comes from the Book of Isaiah. The prophet Isaiah, speaking to the Israelites, said, "Listen to me, you who pursue deliverance, you who seek the LORD; look to the rock from which you were hewn, and to the quarry from which you were dug. Look to Abraham your father and to Sarah who bore you; for when he was but one I called him, and I blessed him and made him many" (Is 51:1–2). When Isaiah said, "Look to Abraham and Sarah," he was referring to the fact that all of the descendants of Israel (Jacob) can trace their lineage to Abraham and Sarah. Notice how Isaiah used the imagery of the quarry and the rock. This is the background of Jesus's statement, "You are Peter and on this rock I will build my Church." The key focus here is on Jesus, who at this moment is changing Simon's name to "Rock." And Jesus is going to build on this rock, thus giving us the image of *Christus faber* (Christ the builder).

Toward the end of the Sermon on the Mount in Matthew's Gospel, Jesus tells his disciples that the wise man will not only hear his words but will follow them; and that those who follow his words will be like the wise man who built his house on rock. Here, Jesus is the builder, and he is building on Peter—and by building on Peter, Jesus is the wise man. Of course, Solomon was the wise man *par excellence* in the Old Testament. While Solomon was known for a lot of things, by far his most important accomplishment was building the Temple in Jerusalem. And he built his Temple on a rock—called the *Eben Shetiya* in Jewish tradition. In

Hebrew *eben* means "stone" or "rock," and the *Eben Shetiya* was the foundation stone of the Temple. The Old Testament also tells us that Solomon built the Temple on Mount Moriah (*cf.* 2 Chr 3:1–3), which is the same rock upon which Abraham offered his son Isaac, almost sacrificing him before God sent an angel to stop him. So Solomon, a wise man, built God's house, the temple or house *par excellence*, on the same rock upon which Abraham almost sacrificed Isaac. Now Jesus turns to Peter and says, "You are Peter and on this rock I will build my Church," my Temple, my house *par excellence*. However, this foundation will be a living stone—a "rock" only metaphorically speaking.

It is significant to note that Herod the Great, who was Edomite and not Jewish, had to travel all the way to Rome to be crowned king of the Jews by Caesar Augustus. The Jews despised him, which caused constant turmoil during his reign. So Herod, in order to legitimize his kingship, decided to build a better Temple than that of Solomon. He dismantled the smaller Temple that Jeremiah had helped rebuild, expanded the Temple platform to thirty-one acres, and began one of the most massive building projects of antiquity. At one time during its construction, there were over 10,000 men working on the Temple. The first-century Jewish historian Josephus tells us that Herod wanted to show that he was the true messiah, the coming king, and the new Solomon, who would restore Israel and the kingdom.

Then there is Jesus, also a king and a builder. He had just been proclaimed messiah or king by Peter, and he declared his first royal act would be to build, and he chose Peter for the foundation. As we reflect on this story, we should give thanks for the wisdom of Christ, who builds using living stones, beginning with Peter. We should ask that we, too, become living stones built on the foundation of Christ and the Apostles. We should build our spiritual lives on the rock, so that when the winds come and the storms rage, we will remain firm and steadfast in our faith—that faith built on Peter.

Chapter 5

Peter and the Keys:
The Primacy of the Church

In the last chapter we examined the episode in Matthew's Gospel in which Peter made his profession of faith in Jesus's true identity and then received the keys to the kingdom of Heaven. In that gospel passage, we saw a kind of two-fold revelation in the exchange between Peter and Jesus. Peter revealed something about Jesus: "You are the Christ, the Son of the living God" (Mt 16:16)—and Jesus revealed something about Peter: "Blessed are you, Simon Bar-Jona! ... You are Peter, and on this rock I will build my church" (Mt 16:17–18).

By calling Jesus the "Son of the *living* God," Peter set Jesus apart from a false claimant to this title—the Roman emperor. This would be the start of a clash between Caesar's claim to divinity and Jesus's claim. People would have to choose sides. Looking back at Church history, we know that the allegiance of Christ's followers created a tension that resulted in three centuries of Roman persecution, beginning with the reign of Nero. Thousands of Christians, like Peter, would boldly profess that Jesus was the true Son of the living God. Others, unfortunately, denied Christ, instead giving their allegiance to Caesar and offering him sacrifice.

Jesus also changed Simon's name to Peter (meaning "rock") and said that on this "rock" he would build his Church. Like the kings in the ancient world, Jesus would be a builder who built his house on solid rock. Peter, the passive recipient of Jesus's actions, would be the rock upon which Jesus would build. It is important to realize that Christ was the protagonist of this building project. Jesus had laid the groundwork for this idea of building in the Sermon on the Mount when he spoke about the wise man who built his house on rock. King Solomon, the Old Testament paragon of wisdom, built his Temple on the rock of Mount Moriah, the same rock where Abraham prepared to sacrifice Isaac. This Temple built by Solomon would be the center of Jewish worship for the next thousand years. Jesus would build a "new temple" that would define and establish his kingdom and the royal authority of his dynasty. Unlike the kings of antiquity, however, Jesus was not going to build on a physical rock in a specific place but on the person of Peter. While the Old Covenant had a physical Temple built by Solomon in all of his wisdom, the New Covenant would have a very different kind of temple—Christ himself.

Peter the Rock

The images of Christ as a new temple and Peter as the rock are wonderfully illustrated in the beautiful and theologically rich painting by Pietro Perugino entitled *Delivery of the Keys*. The painting shows a magnificent landscape, which alone makes it a masterpiece of Italian Renaissance art. But even more interesting is what is happening in front of the landscape. Behind the figures of Jesus, Peter, and the others who are gathered around them, there is a building that represents the Jerusalem Temple. Yet, Perugino's rendering of the Temple looks curiously like the building that still occupies the site, a structure built upon the raised foundation seen in the painting—the foundations of the long-gone Temples of Solomon and Herod. Never having visited Jerusalem himself, Perugino painted his Temple based on then-contemporary pilgrims' sketches of the gold-domed, eight-sided Dome of the Rock, the mosque built by Muslims in the seventh century. Perugino also depicts other buildings that wouldn't have been there at the time of Christ but which pilgrims would have seen and sketched, such as Constantine's triumphal arch.

Directly in front of these "modern" buildings—i.e., circa fifteenth-century Jerusalem modern—Perugino shows Jesus giving the keys to Peter. Note that this is not taking place in Caesarea Philippi, where the actual event took place, but on the Temple Mount. Since Solomon built his Temple on this mount or "rock," the same one upon which Abraham prepared to sacrifice Isaac, this is a symbolically fitting setting for Perugino's painting: for Christ is building his Church—his own holy Temple, if you will—upon the "rock" of Peter. Perugino brilliantly juxtaposed these two rocks: that of Abraham's sacrifice and Solomon's Temple in the background and that of Peter in the foreground.

The theological significance of the painting is even more poignant because the painting is displayed in the Sistine Chapel, where cardinals gather to elect a new pope as successor of Peter. Following his election in the last conclave, Pope Francis would have sat looking directly at that painting. This is another example of how Catholic art is

Delivery of the Keys by Perugino

never simply decorative. It's theological and catechetical. Just as in Perugino's painting, it's always teaching us something important about the Faith.

After saying, "You are Peter, and on this rock I will build my Church," Jesus continued, "and the gates of Hades shall not prevail against it" (Mt 16:18). The word translated as "gates of Hades" is also rendered "death" or "gates of Hell" in other English translations. These words are a sort a code for the "powers of Hell." We see this frequently in Scripture. For example, out of respect for the divine name, pious Jews would say "Heaven" instead of "God." In the New Testament, "kingdom of Heaven" is often used in place of "kingdom of God," although the meaning is exactly the same. In this case, Jesus didn't want to give Satan the honor of being named, so he used a circumlocution. Instead of saying "Satan," Jesus referred to him as the "gates of Hades." This is a great promise. Peter would be the foundation of a new kingdom—the Church—and the gates of Hell would not be able to withstand it. There is a great power endowed in this new temple.

Remember that David's kingdom had been conquered and his descendants exiled. The great Solomonic Temple had been destroyed by the Babylonians in 587 BC, and even the Temple built by Herod the Great, still standing at the time of Christ, would be destroyed by the Romans in AD 70. Jesus was saying that he is the new Temple, and that his Temple would be greater than Solomon's Temple. He would lay a foundation stone that would not be overturned. Understanding how this relates to David and the Solomonic Temple helps us to understand Christ as the New David and it helps us to understand the meaning of the new Temple that he built on the rock, which is Peter.

The Keys to the Kingdom

After telling Peter that the powers of death would not prevail against his Church, Jesus said, "I will give you the keys to the kingdom of heaven" (Mt 16:19). What did Christ mean by "the keys to the kingdom of heaven"? We often think of keys to the actual gates of Heaven, which leads to a lot of Catholic jokes. Rather than actual keys that allow people to enter Heaven, Jesus was giving Peter—and his successors—a heavenly authority that would be exercised on earth. Remember the practice of circumlocution. For example, when the prodigal son comes back to his father, he says, "Father,

I have sinned against heaven and before you" (Lk 15:21). What does the son mean when he says he has "sinned against heaven"? Obviously, he means that he has sinned against God. Matthew, as a good and pious Jew, normally uses the term "kingdom of Heaven," whereas Luke or Mark, who are writing to Gentile audiences, more often use the phrase "kingdom of God." When the Old Testament speaks about the kingdom of God, it is referring to Israel. It's not about a kingdom in Heaven; rather, it's referring to a kingdom on earth. For example, when Solomon became king, Scripture tells us that he sat on the throne of the Lord (*cf.* 1 Chr 29:23), not the throne of his father David, as we might expect the verse to say. If we go back a few verses, however, it says:

> David blessed the LORD in the presence of all the assembly; and David said: "Blessed are you, O LORD, the God of Israel our father, for ever and ever. Yours, O LORD, is the greatness, and the power, and the glory, and the victory, and the majesty; for all that is in the heavens and in the earth is yours; yours is the kingdom, O LORD, and you are exalted as head above all." (1 Chr 29:10–11)

In this prayer, David is proclaiming that the kingdom belongs to God and that he is acting as God's steward. That is why he says, "Yours is the greatness, and the power, and the glory, and the victory, and the majesty." It's not David's glory or David's kingdom that he is giving to his son, but God's. David is professing that he is giving the stewardship of God's kingdom to Solomon. The significance of this is that Jesus—as seen in the Nativity stories found in the Gospels of Matthew and Luke—belongs to the line of David. He is coming as the New David, and he is establishing a new kingdom. Now, he is telling Peter that he is giving him the keys to the kingdom. But this doesn't mean that Peter is king. If we go back and examine the Davidic kingdom, we find that there was a person who acted as a sort of prime minister. The king held the authority, but his "prime minister" would be the administrative leader of the kingdom, acting in the name of the king. The Old Testament tells us that this person was given the "key of the house of David" (Is 22:22), which signified his authority to administer the kingdom.

We also see an example of this in a markedly different culture in the Book of Genesis. Pharaoh was the king, but he would have "cabinet" positions, and one of these positions was the steward who was set over the house of Pharaoh. When Joseph interpreted Pharaoh's dreams, Pharaoh acknowledged Joseph's great wisdom and rewarded him, saying:

> "Since God has shown you all this, there is none so discreet and wise as you are; you shall be over my house, and all my people shall order themselves as you command; only as regards the throne will I be greater than you." And Pharaoh said to Joseph, "Behold, I have set you over all the land of Egypt." Then Pharaoh took his signet ring from his hand and put it on Joseph's hand, and arrayed him in garments of fine linen, and put a gold chain about his neck. (Gn 41:39–42)

Pharaoh makes Joseph his "prime minister," and as a sign of his authority over all Egypt, Joseph is given the robe of authority and a signet ring. The particular phrase in Hebrew that is used to describe his authority is that he is over the "house of Pharaoh." Going back a couple of chapters in the Book of Genesis, we see that Joseph had previously been set over the "house of Potiphar," which indicated that he was his chief steward, and, as Joseph said to Potiphar's wife, "He has put everything that he has in my hand" (Gn 39:8). Potiphar was a general of Pharaoh, and it was common practice for the nobility who had large estates with many servants to choose one to act as their chief steward—a sort of modern-day chief operating officer.

One final example comes from the Book of Isaiah, which relates the story of King Hezekiah, a righteous king of Judah. "Thus says the Lord GOD of hosts, 'Come, go to this steward, to Shebna, who is over the household'" (Is 22:15). In Hebrew the phrase translated as "over the household" is *ha al bayyit. Bayyit* means "house," and the phrase is literally "over the house," which is a Hebrew idiom meaning "chief steward," or more appropriately in the case of a kingdom, "prime minister." The background of this story is that King Hezekiah was under threat from the Assyrians who had surrounded Jerusalem. The Assyrian army had already conquered the other villages and cities in the kingdom of Judah, and it looked like Judah would fall next, so Hezekiah was praying for divine assistance. His enemies urged him to surrender, saying they would negotiate with him for his life, but if he didn't surrender, then things would go badly for him. Shebna, the king's "prime minister," looked at matters from a worldly perspective. Expecting defeat and certain death, he paid the workers to carve out a nice tomb for himself. It was clear that the "prime minister" didn't expect victory, so God was angry and sent his prophet, Isaiah, with an oracle against Shebna:

> "Come, go to this steward, to Shebna, who is over the household, and say to him: What have you to do here and whom have you here, that you have hewn here a tomb for yourself, you who hew a tomb on the height, and carve a habitation for yourself in the rock? Behold, the Lord will hurl you away violently, O you strong man. He will seize firm hold on you, and whirl you round and round, and throw you like a ball into a wide land; there you shall die." (Is 22:15–18)

Basically, God was saying that Shebna would not die in Jerusalem and be buried in a beautiful tomb like he had planned. Rather, he would die in exile because he didn't trust in the Lord. Then, the oracle continued, stating that the Lord would strip Shebna of his office:

> "I will thrust you from your office, and you will be cast down from your station. In that day I will call my servant Eli'akim the son of Hilki'ah, and I will clothe him with your robe, and will bind your belt on him, and will commit your authority to his hand; and he shall be a father to the inhabitants of Jerusalem and to the house of Judah." (Is 22:19–21)

Notice the significance of the office, which plays an important role in this story. It is because of the authority of the office that Eliakim will "be a father to the inhabitants of Jerusalem and to the house of Judah" (Is 22:21). The house of Judah refers to the kingdom of Hezekiah, so the "prime minister" is a type of *father*. In other words, in the kingdom of David the "prime minister's" role was to be a spiritual father. This is why the successors of Peter are called popes, because *pope* means "father." The office of pope is the office of the "prime minister" for Christ the King, and, therefore, the pope acts as spiritual father to all in Christ's kingdom.

The Power to Bind and Loose

The oracle continues, "And I will place on his [Eliakim's] shoulder the key of the house of David; he shall open, and none shall shut; and he shall shut, and none shall open" (Is 22:22). This phraseology is nearly identical to the words that Jesus spoke to Peter in Matthew: "I will give you the keys of the kingdom of heaven, and whatever you bind on earth shall be bound in heaven, and whatever you loose on earth shall be loosed in heaven" (Mt 16:19). What are these keys that Jesus was giving to Peter? The Gospel tells us that these are the keys to the kingdom of Heaven. Binding and loosing literally refers to the authority to arrest and the authority to pardon. This literal understanding is important because many non-Catholics want to metaphorically interpret Jesus's words to mean that the Gospel will free people from sin. However, these words have a precise meaning within Jewish tradition.

In Jewish writings from the eighth century and after, the idea of binding and loosing refers to the authority of a rabbi in the synagogue. If you were to apply this later rabbinical authority to the time of the New Testament, you might be tempted to say that Christ was referring to the Church's authority to make decisions and to pass rulings on ecclesiastical matters. The problem is that these writings from AD 900 and later were made centuries after the time of Christ and reflected a considerable change in rabbinical thought following the destruction of the Temple in AD 70. However, the Judaism of Jesus's day still had the Temple, and the Jews were still waiting expectantly for a king to come and rule over them as a nation. In this gospel episode, Jesus is a king who is re-establishing the Davidic kingdom, so we should expect its structure to mirror that of David's kingdom—and in this kingdom he is placing Peter in the office of "prime minister." So "binding and loosing" refers to something very specific in the context from which Jesus is speaking.

The first-century Jewish historian, Josephus, in *The War of the Jews*, refers to this concept of "binding and loosing." Recounting the Maccabean reign, he mentions one of the Maccabean women who was ruling at the time:

> Now Alexandra hearkened to them, that is to a group of Pharisees, to an extraordinary degree, as being herself a woman of great piety towards God, but these Pharisees artfully insinuated themselves into her favor by little and little, and became themselves the real administrators of the public affairs; they banished and they reduced whom they pleased; they bound and they loosed at their pleasure, and to say all at once, they had the enjoyment of royal authority. (1:111)

Notice the words that Josephus chooses here. He uses the term "bind and loose" to describe the royal authority that had been given to the Pharisees. As we can see from these examples in Scripture and history, the words "binding and loosing" refer to royal authority over the kingdom. This is especially true when we consider the next words in the verse, which tell us that Christ is giving Peter the keys to the "kingdom of Heaven."

Christ the Suffering King

Following this grant of authority to Peter, Jesus instructed the disciples to tell no one that he was the Christ—the Anointed One, the king—because it was politically dangerous. Rome was in charge, and Herod was a client king of Rome. Both Herod and the emperor were fiercely jealous of anyone who made royal claims. In fact, when Christ did publicly accept the title of king and make his triumphant entry into Jerusalem, he was crucified within a week. And the crime he was accused of committing was claiming to be the "King of the Jews." As if to emphasize this danger, a few verses after the scene in which Christ gave Peter the keys, Jesus explained to his disciples that he must go to Jerusalem, where he would suffer at the hands of the Jewish authorities and be put to death.

What a change in the conversation. Jesus had just spoken about establishing his new kingdom and just appointed a prime minister. Now he was saying that he was going to Jerusalem to be killed. This was certainly not what Peter and the disciples expected Jesus to say next. Christ went on to say that he would die and on the third day he would rise again. At this point, Peter began to rebuke him, saying, "God forbid, Lord! This shall never happen to you" (Mt 16:22). Peter invoked the Father in Heaven, who had revealed to him that

Jesus was the Christ, the Son of the living God. He invoked God as an authority to stop Jesus from going to Jerusalem to suffer death. Previously, Peter made a revelation about Jesus, and the Lord made a revelation in return. Here, Peter rebukes Jesus and Jesus rebukes him back, declaring to Peter, "Get behind me, Satan! You are a hindrance to me; for you are not on the side of God, but of men" (Mt 16:23). Peter had just received a great office with tremendous authority, and it went straight to his head. He was already trying to take charge of the king. Peter was bluntly reminded that while he may be "prime minister," Christ was still king.

Let's examine the verse, "Get behind me, Satan!" in more detail. The word *satan* means "adversary," so Jesus was telling Peter not to be his adversary. Basically, "Don't put yourself in the place of Satan by opposing me." Next, he told Peter that he was a "hindrance" to him and that he was "not on the side of God, but of men." In other words, he was saying that Peter had a worldly perspective about the coming kingdom. To be fair, all of the disciples had a worldly view of the Messiah's reign, as did all of Israel. However, it's interesting to note that Peter took notice of Jesus's rebuke and changed. When we examine Peter's preaching in the Acts of the Apostles and his letters in the New Testament, we find Peter proclaiming most emphatically that Jesus had to suffer and die in accordance with the prophets. Jesus was rough on Peter because he needed Peter to go through a *metanoia*, a transformation in his thinking about what it meant for Jesus to be the king and Messiah of the kingdom, i.e., to shift from a human, political perspective to God's perspective.

> Then Jesus told his disciples, "If any man would come after me, let
> him deny himself and take up his cross and follow me. For whoever
> would save his life will lose it, and whoever loses his life for my sake
> will find it. For what will it profit a man, if he gains the whole world
> and forfeits his life? Or what shall a man give in return for his life?"
> (Mt 16:24–26)

Jesus didn't tell his disciples to put their crosses aside
because he was going to die for them and they wouldn't
have to suffer. That's the "health and wealth" gospel, but
it's not the Gospel of Jesus Christ. God calls us to conform
ourselves to Jesus Christ, which means that we have to suffer trials and tribulations in this world. The glory will come
later in Heaven.

Peter would end up embracing this true discipleship.
He would take up his cross, he would follow Christ, and he
would give up his life. But, at this point in the story, Peter still
has to learn, and this takes us back to the beginning of the
story, in Bethsaida, when Jesus healed the blind man in two
stages. After Bethsaida, Jesus took his disciples to Caesarea
Phillipi and asked them who the people thought that he
was. Peter answered correctly that Jesus was "the Christ, the
Son of the living God," but he didn't yet understand what
it meant for him to be the Messiah. Peter still thought that
the Messiah would be a triumphant king—a worldly king.
He didn't understand that Jesus was going to be a suffering
king who would give his life as a ransom for sins. He was
not going to be a political king who would liberate his people
from the domination of the Romans; he is a king who will

liberate all mankind from the domination of Satan and the sin that occupies our hearts. But to do this, he had to die as ransom for our sins.

While Peter's inspired revelation of Jesus's identity was correct, he was still myopic. Like the blind man whom Jesus healed, Peter needed his vision cured in two stages. In the first, he saw partially that Jesus was indeed the Messiah, the Son of the living God. But it wouldn't be until the second stage that he would see that Jesus must die on the Cross to save us, and that is when Jesus would be enthroned as a king *par excellence.*

Like Peter, we often have to go through these stages as disciples of Christ. We think that once we have come close to God that we're going to be safe and protected. We expect to prosper and believe that everything will be great, but then we have a crisis and are scandalized, wondering why we must suffer. It's because we follow a crucified Lord, and his discipleship takes a cruciform shape. But this is part of God's blessing. He who gives up his life will find it because it profits us nothing to gain the whole world if we lose our soul. These are the incredible words that Jesus gives us. We should ask God that, like Peter, we may have our vision corrected so that we can see the truth of Christ's kingship and the beauty of his power, which is made manifest in weakness, and that we may be enabled to pick up our own daily crosses and follow him in hope and faith.

Chapter 6

In the Shadow of the Galilean:
Peter's Rising Leadership

In the last chapter, we saw how Jesus made Peter his "prime minister" and gave him the keys of the kingdom of Heaven. Peter had been "deputized" by Christ to lead the Church in his absence. Having "passed the baton," so to speak, Jesus spoke about his upcoming Passion and Death. Now that he had prepared the way for succession, Jesus was basically saying he was ready to die.

When studying the kingdom of David in the Old Testament, it's interesting to note that whenever the king was absent or gone, the "prime minister" (*ha al bayyit* in Hebrew) would rule in his place. An example of this can be found in Second Kings where the king contracted leprosy (*cf.* 15:5). Under the Mosaic Law, the king was declared unclean and banished from the city. In his absence, the king's son was appointed "prime minister" and administered the kingdom. Because the king hadn't died yet, the son couldn't become king, but as prime minister was given all of the authority of the king. He ruled as prime minister until his father died and then was crowned king. From this and other Old Testament stories, you can see the biblical foundation of this office of "prime minister" that Jesus sets up in his new kingdom. Jesus knew he was going to be crucified and that he would return to his Father in Heaven, so he made a plan for the Church to be led in his absence.

The Importance of the Kingdom

This leads to a bigger question: "Why did Jesus die?" Most people, on first thought, would probably answer that Jesus died to save us from our sins. The problem with this answer is that it reduces the entire mission of Jesus Christ to doing just one thing. While it is certainly correct in and of itself, it's not the whole answer. If dying for our sins was the extent of his mission, then he could have accomplished it just as easily by dying as an infant when Herod sent his soldiers to kill "all the male children in Bethlehem and in all that region who were two years old or under" (Mt 2:16). A person might reply that Jesus had to be put to death as an adult in order to show that he chose to die freely. If this were the case, then he could have died in Nazareth following his first homily when the people were so angry that they wanted to throw him off the cliff (*cf.* Lk 4:16–30). Or someone might answer that he had to die in Jerusalem in order to fulfill the prophets. Yet, we have the instance where Jesus was in Jerusalem and said, "Truly, truly, I say to you, before Abraham was, I am" (Jn 8:58). The crowd was so angry that they started looking for stones to throw. Meanwhile, Jesus left and escaped through the crowd.

In fact, the Gospels show us that Jesus escaped death over and over again. In fact, he was so discrete with his itinerary that Peter and the Apostles didn't know day-to-day where they would be going. They traveled from village to village and often through fields rather than the main roads. Why was Jesus so elusive? The reason is that the last prophet before him—John the Baptist—was killed. Even when Jesus gave Peter the keys and spoke of his upcoming Death, he told them to keep quiet for the time being. Even on the day of Passover Jesus didn't tell the disciples where they were going to celebrate the Passover meal. Why all of the elusiveness about the Passover meal even among his disciples? Jesus knew that Judas was going to betray him, but he still had something left to accomplish before he died. If Judas knew where the Passover was going to be celebrated, then he would have informed the Jewish authorities, and Jesus would have been arrested before having a chance to celebrate the Last Supper—the ritual meal in which he instituted the Sacraments of the Eucharist and Holy Orders.

In other words, we cannot reduce the entire mission of Jesus to just his Death. While his Death was certainly the climax of his life, you cannot take it out of the context of his entire life without diminishing that event itself. Such an approach minimizes the importance of his teachings, his miracles, and the many things that he needed to accomplish before his Death—including the significant event of establishing the kingdom on Peter, "the rock."

What does Christ say? "You are Peter, and on this rock I will build my Church" (Mt 16:18). Jesus didn't come only to die but to build his kingdom. He died not only to "save us *from*" our sins but to "save us *for*" the kingdom that he was going to establish—to be part of his family, the kingdom of

God, the *basileia tou theou*. This is why he didn't speak about his Death until he gave the keys to Peter—he had to prepare the succession for his kingdom. Moreover, as soon as he gave the keys to Peter—way up north in Caesarea Philippi—Jesus started heading south toward Jerusalem. Basically, once Peter had the keys, Jesus had laid the foundation for the kingdom and established succession, so he began his journey to Jerusalem where he was to die.

It is unfortunate that many people say something to the effect: "I believe in Jesus; just not in the Church." One time a friend asked me to speak with her brother, who had decided to leave the Catholic Church. When I spoke with him, he told me, "I still believe in Jesus; it's just the Church that I don't believe in anymore." I asked him, "What was the main thing that Jesus spoke about in the Gospels?" He quickly replied, "Love." However, he couldn't point to any verse in the Bible where Jesus actually spoke about love. In all fairness, the New Testament does speak plenty about loving God the Father, about loving Jesus Christ, and about loving others as ourselves. Certainly, love is an important part of Jesus's message, but it's not the only part or even the issue Jesus spoke about the most. Rather, the dominant topic of Jesus's teachings is the kingdom of God (Heaven). If you look at his parables, most of them are about the kingdom. For example, Jesus will say:

- "The kingdom of heaven is like a grain of mustard seed which a man took and sowed in his field" (Mt 13:31);
- "The kingdom of heaven is like leaven which a woman took and hid in three measures of meal, till it was all leavened" (Mt 13:33);

- "The kingdom of heaven is like treasure hidden in a field" (Mt 13:44); and
- "The kingdom of heaven is like a merchant in search of fine pearls" (Mt 13:45).

These are just a few examples from Matthew's Gospel that show us Jesus was a king who was always teaching about his kingdom. We can't lose sight of this important fact.

If we really want to learn about Jesus's mission, then we need to look closely at what he does before he dies. In fact, one of the many good reasons to study Peter is because it gives us so much information about Jesus and his mission. The fact that Peter was given the keys and was chosen to be the foundation upon which Jesus will build tells us a lot about Christ and his kingdom.

The Transfiguration

In addition to the Gospel episode about the keys, there are two other scenes later in the Gospels that tell us something very significant about Jesus. The first of these two scenes is the Transfiguration of Christ on Mount Tabor. In Luke's Gospel, we read, "Now about eight days after these sayings he took with him Peter and John and James, and went up on the mountain to pray" (Lk 9:28). The fact that Jesus took three Apostles with him is highly significant. We are used to hearing about the Twelve. In fact, by choosing twelve Apostles, Jesus showed that he was establishing the New Israel. In a sense, Jesus is the new Jacob—later given the new name of Israel—whose twelve sons became the patriarchs of the Twelve Tribes of Israel. Just as Jacob had twelve sons, Jesus had twelve Apostles.

Jesus is also the New David who gave the keys to Peter and established him as the "prime minister" of the kingdom—an office also found in the Davidic kingdom. In a similar way, when we study the figure of Moses, we see that when he went up on Mount Sinai he took three men (Aaron and Aaron's two sons, Nadab and Abihu) who formed an inner circle around Moses. They even participated in a type of covenant meal with the Lord (*cf.* Ex 24:9–11). This inner circle of three Apostles suggests that Jesus is the New Moses and the New David.

We will see Peter, James, and John again with Jesus when he heals Jairus's daughter and later in the Garden of Gethsemane. It's significant that Peter, who is always listed first among the Twelve, is also listed first among the inner circle. This inner circle of Apostles, who had privileged access to Jesus and his teachings, will later write the New Testament epistles of James, Peter, and John, which, along with the letters of Paul, are especially authoritative because they were written by Apostles who shared an especially close relationship with Christ. In a sense, Jesus was preparing these three to lead the Twelve, who together would lead the Church.

In Exodus, we read how Moses took Aaron, Nadab, and Abihu further up the mountain, leaving the rest of Israel down below. At Mount Tabor, Jesus, the new Moses, took Peter, James, and John further up the mountain, leaving the other nine Apostles down below. Scripture tells us that "as he was praying, the appearance of his countenance was altered, and his clothing became dazzling white. And behold, two men talked with him, Moses and Eli'jah, who appeared in glory and spoke of his exodus, which he was to accomplish at Jerusalem" (Lk 9:29–31).

"As the men were parting from him, Peter said to Jesus, 'Master, it is well that we are here; let us make three booths, one for you and one for Moses and one for Eli'jah'—not knowing what he said" (Lk 9:33). Some biblical commentaries will say that the "three booths" refer to tents and illustrate Peter's desire to stay up on the mountain. There is some truth to that, but the deeper meaning of Peter's words comes out of his experience. The Gospel of Luke tells us that the Transfiguration occurred "about eight days after these sayings" (Lk 9:28)—i.e., the mutual revelations of Peter and Jesus, at which Christ gave his "rock" the keys to the kingdom of Heaven. The number eight is significant because the Jewish Feast of Tabernacles—also known as *Sukkoth*, meaning "booths"—lasts eight days. During the Feast of Tabernacles or Feast of Booths, the Jews to this day set up booths, which are similar to little three-sided houses. The booths only had three walls because they weren't permanent; they represented the tents in which the Israelites lived during their sojourn to the Promised Land. The purpose of the feast was for the Jews to relive the Exodus desert experience and to recall how God provided for Israel in the wilderness and gave the gift of the Law on Mount Sinai.

In this instance, Jesus takes his inner circle up the mountain to pray—most likely during the Feast of Booths. That is why Peter likely thought of building booths and why the idea is not as odd as it might sound to our modern ears. The Transfiguration is a replay of what happened on Mount Sinai—the event that is celebrated in the Feast of Booths. On both Mount Sinai and Mount Tabor, a cloud came down on the mountains and a voice from Heaven spoke. Whereas on Mount Sinai, the voice spoke and gave the Law to Moses, on Mount Tabor, the voice revealed the new law, which is not a list of commandments but rather the Person of Christ himself.

"As he said this, a cloud came and overshadowed them; and they were afraid as they entered the cloud. And a voice came out of the cloud, saying, 'This is my Son, my Chosen; listen to him!'" (Lk 9:34–35). There are two parts to this revelation of the Father. "This is my Son, my Chosen," evokes Genesis 22, in which Abraham was asked to sacrifice Isaac, his only son. On Mount Tabor Jesus was preparing to go to Jerusalem where he was to be sacrificed on the Cross as the only beloved Son of the Father. "Chosen" is the same word used in Isaiah 42:1 in reference to a suffering servant. This is followed by the second part of the revelation, "Listen to him." *Shema* is the Hebrew word used in the Old Testament to indicate listening. In the famous *Shema Yisrael* ("Hear, O Israel"), the people of Israel were summoned to hear and obey the covenant they had received (*cf.* Dt 6:4). In Deuteronomy 18:18, Moses foretold that God would send another prophet like himself who would administer a new covenant—and Moses told Israel that they must listen (*shema*) to him. So when God the Father said that Jesus is his Son, his Chosen, and gives the command to listen to him, he was giving testimony that Jesus is the prophet foretold by Moses. Thus, the story of the Transfiguration makes perfect sense when you view Jesus as the new Moses, the new lawgiver, and Peter as the new Aaron, the new high priest.

Peter's Takeaway from the Transfiguration

The revelation given by God the Father in the Transfiguration was formative for Peter. Remember how incomprehensibly abhorrent the prospect of Jesus's Death was to him. Here at the Transfiguration, at the outset of the journey to Jerusalem where Jesus will die, Peter and the Apostles were being prepared for the Crucifixion. They were given a glimpse of Jesus's glory before his Death, which was to help prepare them and strengthen them for the way of the Cross. In fact, the Transfiguration was so formative for Peter that he mentioned it in his Second Letter.

> For we did not follow cleverly devised myths when we made known to you the power and coming of our Lord Jesus Christ, but we were eyewitnesses of his majesty. For when he received honor and glory from God the Father and the voice was borne to him by the Majestic Glory, "This is my beloved Son, with whom I am well pleased," we heard this voice borne from heaven, for we were with him on the holy mountain. (2 Pt 1:16–18)

In the last line Peter is clearly referring to the Transfiguration. He continues, "And we have the prophetic word made more sure. You will do well to pay attention to this as to a lamp shining in a dark place, until the day dawns and the morning star rises in your hearts" (2 Pt 1:19). Peter was telling the community that they would have to suffer and walk through this valley of tears, darkness, and pain, but the revelation from the Father would be a lamp to light their path. The truth of Christ's suffering and Death, followed by his glory, will help us as we walk through our own *Via Dolorosa* (Way of the Cross). Just as Christ was glorified, our own glory awaits if we persevere. In this way, Peter was teaching the early Church, which was beginning to suffer persecution, that Jesus is the model for suffering and the glory that follows.

"His divine power has granted to us all things that pertain to life and godliness, through the knowledge of him who called us to his own glory and excellence" (1 Pt 1:3). Peter, who witnessed this glory of Jesus, tells us that we, too, are called to this same glory "by which he has granted to us his precious and very great promises, that through these you may escape from the corruption that is in the world because of passion, and become partakers of the divine nature" (1 Pt 1:4). In the Transfiguration, Peter saw not only the divine nature of Jesus but also the glory of Elijah and Moses. Peter realized that the glory of God is poured out on all who are called by him and who follow him. This partaking in the divine nature and participation in the divine glory is what we are called to share in as Christians. What Christ has, we will share in—and this includes both his suffering and his glory. These are inseparable. You cannot have the glory without the suffering.

Peter's experience of the Transfiguration became for him a lamp shining in the darkness, which gave him great light and hope in the midst of great tribulation. One of the many reasons we know this to be true is because Peter wrote his

Second Letter from prison in Rome, a very dark place indeed. This is how the Church and each of us should hold on to the sufferings and glorification of Christ—as a lamp that lights up the darkness in our own time.

Taxes

Looking at the Transfiguration in Matthew's Gospel, we see that after they came down from the mountain, they encountered a man with a son who had seizures, whom Jesus healed. Following this, they went back to Galilee. "When they came to Caper'naum, the collectors of the half-shekel tax went up to Peter and said, 'Does not your teacher pay the tax?'" (Mt 17:24). The historical background is that Moses had commanded every male, upon reaching twenty years of age, to pay a half-shekel tax to the sanctuary. This had been part of Jewish tradition for centuries, and in itself was not controversial. The controversy over the tax only began when Herod the Great rebuilt the Temple. This building project, at one time utilizing over 10,000 workers, was extraordinarily expensive. While the Pharisees and chief priests didn't like Herod, they cooperated with him in rebuilding the Temple because they thought, once the Temple was finished, God would come and re-establish the kingdom. So, to help Herod pay for the rebuilding of the Temple, the Pharisees reinterpreted the Law of Moses to require the payment of the half-shekel tax each and every year rather than just once in a man's life. Now, every male over twenty had to pay the tax every single year, and this became controversial.

The Essenes, a group of very devout Jews, argued that this interpretation was not what Moses had commanded and accused the Pharisees of changing the Law. They refused to pay the tax because they saw the priesthood as having become corrupted. With this background, we can see the importance of the question. The Pharisees believed that the tax was important because it would be the impetus to the arrival of the messiah who would save the nation. The Essenes saw the yearly tax as a corruption of the Law. So the question was really about what side Jesus would take in this controversy. Where did he stand on this issue theologically? This is exactly the type of theological question that would have been discussed in first-century Israel.

Peter didn't know the answer to the question, so the prudent thing would have been for him to ask Jesus. However, the pre-Pentecost Peter was usually not very prudent. Not wanting to upset the tax collectors, he immediately answered that Jesus pays the tax. Having committed Jesus to paying the tax, he then had to go home and tell Jesus what he had done. As soon as he returned, Jesus spoke with him first, calling him "Simon," instead of "Peter."

> "What do you think, Simon? From whom do kings of the earth take toll or tribute? From their sons or from others?" And when he said, "From others," Jesus said to him, "Then the sons are free. However, not to give offense to them, go to the sea and cast a hook, and take the first fish that comes up, and when you open its mouth you will find a shekel; take that and give it to them for me and for yourself."
> (Mt 17:25–27)

In the modern world, we view taxes as a bureaucratic or legal matter. However, in the ancient world, especially in Israel, taxes were a theological issue. When a king claimed to have a royal right to kingship over a nation, he would demand tribute. Therefore, paying tribute was an act of allegiance to that king. This is why paying taxes to Caesar was so controversial, because it indicated that you recognized his right to rule Israel. By paying Caesar, you were in effect denying that God was the ultimate ruler of Israel and that his anointed king had to be from the line of David. Paying taxes to the king, then, also became a theological question.

It's significant that, in the ancient world, kings and the sons of kings were free from paying taxes. In Israel, this privilege was even extended to the high priest and his family, who were exempt from paying taxes to the Greeks and the Romans. Jesus was claiming to be the king, yet, if he paid the tax, it signified his recognition that there was an earthly authority over him.

Jesus's answer reminded Peter that he was the king and that he did not have to pay the tax. But to avoid giving offense, he directed Peter to pay it. Remember the keys? What Peter binds on earth will be bound in Heaven, and that is exactly what happened here. Peter had committed Jesus to paying the tax, and so Jesus paid it.

Notice that Jesus didn't say that Peter would find six and a half shekels in the fish to pay the tax for Jesus and all of the Apostles. Rather, there was only to be one shekel, for Jesus and Peter. Only Jesus and Peter—the king and the "prime minister"—were exempt. The others must pay for themselves.

Even after rebuking Peter, Jesus confirmed that he is the New Jonah and that Peter is the Bar-Jonah ("son of Jonah"). This further illustrates the relationship that Peter had with Jesus and the authority that he had received from him.

This practice of exemption of the Church from taxes has always been the tradition of Christendom. The Church does not pay a tax because it is the *basileia tou theou*, the kingdom of God, which transcends this world and is above all earthly kingdoms. In this sense, the tax exemption of the Church is not just a nice overture from the government that places it on par with other not-for-profit corporations. Rather, it is a theological claim that recognizes the kingship of Jesus Christ.

Entering Jerusalem

The significance of the Transfiguration was to prepare the Apostles for Jesus's journey to Jerusalem where he would be crucified. It was during this journey that Jesus taught the disciples what they should do in his absence. As we approach Jerusalem—where Peter, as usual, had a key role—we will look at his triumphal entry into the city on what we now call Palm Sunday. This event inaugurates the preparation for Jesus's Passion.

> And when they drew near to Jerusalem, to Beth'phage and Beth'any, at the Mount of Olives, he sent two of his disciples, and said to them, "Go into the village opposite you, and immediately as you enter it you will find a colt tied, on which no one has ever sat; untie it and bring it. If any one says to you, 'Why are you doing this?' say,

'The Lord has need of it and will send it back here immediately.'"
(Mk 11:1–3)

Luke's Gospel tells us the names of these two Apostles—
Peter and John. So Jesus sent Peter out to find a colt. According
to the Mosaic Law, you couldn't just claim someone's colt by
saying that your lord had need of it. In this case, however, the
Lord in question is Jesus, who is the king, and the king does
have the right to sequester his subject's property if there is a
pressing need. By claiming the colt for his triumphal entrance
into Jerusalem, Jesus was exercising his royal authority.

> They brought the colt to Jesus, and threw their garments on it;
> and he sat upon it. And many spread their garments on the road,
> and others spread leafy branches which they had cut from the
> fields. And those who went before and those who followed cried
> out, "Hosanna! Blessed is he who comes in the name of the Lord!
> Blessed is the kingdom of our father David that is coming! Hosanna
> in the highest!" (Mk 11:7–10)

The crowd sings "Blessed is the kingdom of our father
David." This is from Psalm 1:18, although the word "David"
has been added. The reason for this addition is that Mark was
writing to a Gentile audience, so he needed to be specific as to
exactly which kingdom he was speaking about.

By entering Jerusalem on a colt, Jesus was following the
exact specifications that David gave to his son, Solomon, for
his coronation. This also fulfilled the prophecy of Zechariah,
who foretold, "Rejoice greatly, O daughter of Zion! Shout
aloud, O daughter of Jerusalem! Behold, your king comes

to you; triumphant and victorious is he, humble and riding on a donkey, on a colt the foal of a donkey" (Zech 9:9). As a king, Jesus is exceedingly humble. Notice that he entered Jerusalem on a colt and not on the war horse of a conquering hero. While this was a sign of humility for Jesus, it would not have been humble for anyone else but a king since pilgrims were required to walk into Jerusalem and to the Temple. Jesus, however, was arriving for his coronation, and so rode humbly on a colt.

The crowds throw down their garments, which is an act of anointing—an act of coronation. They are proclaiming Jesus as king. If we look at 2 Kings 9:3, we see Jehu was made king and anointed by the prophet Elisha. When the people learned of this, every man took off his robe and threw it down for Jehu to walk over. This was a sign of submission and acknowledgment of his kingship. In like manner, Palm Sunday was the first public acknowledgment of Jesus's kingship. He rode a colt like Solomon, and the people threw down their garments as was done for Jehu. They also waved palm branches, which are a sign of victory. They saw Jesus as a king—and he'll be crucified within days under the charge of claiming to be the king of the Jews.

The Last Supper

This takes us to the twenty-second chapter of Luke's Gospel, which concerns the Last Supper that Jesus would celebrate with his Apostles before being crucified. We are told that "the feast of Unleavened Bread drew near, which is called the Passover" (Lk 22:1). The chief priests had been plotting with Judas to betray Jesus, but they didn't want to make their move during the Passover.

> Then came the day of Unleavened Bread, on which the Passover lamb had to be sacrificed. So Jesus sent Peter and John, saying, "Go and prepare the passover for us, that we may eat it." They said to him, "Where will you have us prepare it?" He said to them, "Behold, when you have entered the city, a man carrying a jar of water will meet you; follow him into the house which he enters, and tell the householder, 'The Teacher says to you, Where is the guest room, where I am to eat the Passover with my disciples?' And he will show you a large upper room furnished; there make ready." And they went, and found it as he had told them; and they prepared the passover. (Lk 22:7–13)

When the hour had come, Jesus gathered all of the Apostles for the Passover meal, the Last Supper. Notice that once again Peter and John are the main actors. In the verses that follow, which we'll examine in detail in the next chapter, we'll see the important role of Peter continues.

The Church and the Kingdom

As we've seen from examining the events that occurred from the Transfiguration through the triumphal entrance into Jerusalem, we can't simply reduce the purpose of Jesus's earthly life to his Death. While he did come to save us from our sins, Jesus had much to accomplish before he died—and the best evidence of this is Peter. When Jesus gave Peter the keys, he established a kingdom. Notice that when he told Peter that he is the rock on which he is going to build his Church, the terms "Church" and "kingdom" are synonymous.

Remember the earlier story of my conversation with the young man who said he still believed in Jesus, just not in the Church? You can't separate the king from his kingdom. Or, in other words, you can't separate Jesus from his Church. You can't be loyal to the king if you don't submit to his kingdom. Rather, you must be faithful to and love those to whom the king has given authority in the kingdom. In regard to the followers of Christ, this means that you can't be loyal to Christ if you don't submit to his Church: if you aren't faithful to and love those to whom Jesus has given authority in his Church, then you're not being faithful to him.

The question, "Isn't Jesus enough?" is a great question, but, following the common practice of the rabbis in Jesus's time, it's helpful to answer a question with a question. In this case, the follow-up question is, "Can you be loyal to the king without being loyal to his kingdom?" The young man in my conversation truthfully answered that in all his years as a Catholic, he had never realized the connection between the two.

Having examined the journey of Christ from the Transfiguration to Jerusalem, we're now ready to look at the Passion of Christ and the consummation of his kingdom. We should ask God to help us see the meaning and mystery of the kingdom and to strengthen us so that we might be as faithful to the kingdom as was Peter.

Chapter 7

Discipleship at a Distance:
Peter and the Passion of Christ

At the end of the last chapter, we saw Peter and the other disciples preparing for the Passover meal. As he neared the climax of his ministry, Jesus gathered his Apostles to share a final meal with them. The gospel scenes that follow are rich in meaning, so I want to take a closer look at several of them, especially as they relate to Peter.

Prayers for Peter at the Last Supper

"And when the hour came, [Jesus] sat at table, and the apostles with him. And he said to them, 'I have earnestly desired to eat this Passover with you before I suffer; for I tell you I shall not eat it until it is fulfilled in the kingdom of God'" (Lk 22:14–16). Following these verses, Luke gives us a description of the Last Supper: the meal, the cup, the breaking of the bread, and the conversation that Jesus had with the Twelve. Then we are told that "a dispute also arose among them, which of them was to be regarded as the greatest" (Lk 22:24). Jesus corrected them by saying that the Gentiles seek lordship and glory, but that they were called to serve. "Let the greatest among you become as the youngest, and the leader as one who serves. For which is the greater, one who sits at table, or one who serves? Is it not the one who sits at table? But I am among you as one who serves" (Lk 22:26–27).

And then Jesus gave them a promise: "You are those who have continued with me in my trials; as my Father appointed a kingdom for me, so do I appoint for you that you may eat and drink at my table in my kingdom, and sit on thrones judging the twelve tribes of Israel" (Lk 22:28–30). Once again, we see how focused Jesus was on the kingdom. He then turned to Peter, the leader of the Twelve, and said, "Simon, Simon, behold, Satan demanded to have you, that he might sift you like wheat, but I have prayed for you that your faith may not fail; and when you have turned again, strengthen your brethren" (Lk 22:31–32). The word "turn," which Christ used in this instruction to Peter, comes from the Hebrew word *shuv*, which indicates conversion or repentance. This isn't a conversion in the sense that a nonbeliever becomes a believer. Rather, it is used in the Old Testament sense of Israel going astray and turning back to the Lord. This idea of repentance and turning back occurs many times in the story of Israel. It's this type of conversion to which Jesus was referring when he said to Peter, "When you have turned again, strengthen your brethren." Notice how Jesus, in saying this to Peter, was depending on him to lead the other Apostles.

Peter replied, "Lord, I am ready to go with you to prison and to death" (Lk 22:33). Basically, Peter was telling Jesus that he wouldn't need to "turn again" because he would never turn his back on his Lord. And then Jesus said to him, "I tell you, Peter, the cock will not crow this day, until you three times deny that you know me" (Lk 22:34). Jesus, who knows all things, knew that Peter would deny him, and he was already praying for him—praying that his faith might not fail and that he would strengthen the others. Basically, Jesus was praying for Peter to take on the role of a real leader.

The Garden of Gethsemane

Let's examine this same account in two of the other Gospels. Mark tells us that following the meal, Jesus and the Apostles go to the Garden of Gethsemane, which literally means "the place of the press." "And they went to a place which was called Gethsem'ane; and he said to his disciples, 'Sit here, while I pray.' And he took with him Peter and James and John" (Mk 14:32). Here again, we see this inner circle of three Apostles—Peter, James, and John.

In John's Gospel, we are told that "when Jesus had spoken these words, he went forth with his disciples across the Kidron Valley, where there was a garden, which he and his disciples entered. Now Judas, who betrayed him, also knew the place; for Jesus often met there with his disciples" (Jn 18:1–2). Knowing where Jesus would spend the night, Judas procured a band of soldiers from the chief priests and Pharisees and led them to Jesus so that they could arrest him.

There is a cave in the Garden of Gethsemane called, quite aptly, the Cave of Gethsemane. It is also known as the Cave of Betrayal because that is the exact place where, according to early Christian Tradition, Judas betrayed Jesus. The Cave of Gethsemane is one of my favorite places in the Holy Land because we know that Jesus was there; the Gospel of John tells us that Jesus often stayed in the garden with his disciples. The structural landscape of the Holy Land has undergone dramatic changes over many a tumultuous century, but this cave, now under the care of the Franciscans, remains exactly the same as it was on the night of the Last Supper. Because of this, it is a tremendous and powerful place of prayer. I love to attend Mass in the cave and to have Jesus there with us once again in his Body and Blood.

Archaeologists found an olive press in the cave, which they were able to date to the first century. This is a clear indication that the Garden of Gethsemane was an olive grove and that olives were stored in the cave to be turned by the press into olive oil. It's reasonable to assume that the owner of the olive grove would have been wealthy and that he would have been the person who let Jesus stay in the garden with his disciples.

Interestingly, the Franciscans have put up an icon in the cave, which depicts Jesus meeting Nicodemus in the garden at night. Of course, the third chapter of John's Gospel doesn't tell us exactly where Jesus and Nicodemus met, but it could have been in the cave. It's also worth noting that a man named Nicodemus is mentioned in the Mishna and Talmud—the two central texts of Rabbinic (i.e., post-AD 70) Judaism—as one of the wealthiest men of the time of Christ. They also described him as being righteous and known for his charity. This coincides with the Gospels, which tell us that Nicodemus of Arimathea was a disciple of Jesus and that, when Jesus died, he brought over one hundred pounds of myrrh and spice to anoint his Body—an amount that would have been exceedingly expensive. We also know that Nicodemus defended Jesus when he was brought for trial before the Sanhedrin. For all of these reasons, it's not impossible that Nicodemus, the wealthy disciple of Jesus, was the same Nicodemus who is mentioned in the Mishna and Talmud. If so, perhaps it was his cave where Jesus and his disciples were staying after the Last Supper.

The Gospels tell us that, prior to the Passover, Jesus stayed in Bethany, which is about a mile and a half east of Jerusalem. Why did Jesus go to Gethsemane instead of back to Bethany? The answer can be found in the Jewish Law, which required Jews to celebrate the Passover inside the city of Jerusalem. Jesus, who strictly observed the Law, couldn't cross the Kidron Valley and stay in Bethany. Rather, he spent the night in the Garden of Gethsemane, which was considered part of Jerusalem, most likely staying in the cave. It makes even more sense that Jesus stayed in the garden when we consider that the city was full of pilgrims who had come to Jerusalem for the feast, so there would have been very few places for them to stay. With nowhere to lay his head (*cf.* Lk 9:58), Jesus stayed outside in Gethsemane.

When Jesus arrived at the Garden of Gethsemane, he left nine of his disciples, probably in the Cave of Betrayal, and took Peter, James, and John with him a short distance away. Then he left the three and went a little further into the garden by himself.

And he took with him Peter and James and John, and began to be greatly distressed and troubled. And he said to them, "My soul

is very sorrowful, even to death; remain here, and watch." And
going a little farther, he fell on the ground and prayed that, if it
were possible, the hour might pass from him. And he said, "Abba,
Father, all things are possible to you; remove this chalice from me;
yet not what I will, but what you will." (Mk 14:33–36)

In the Cave of Betrayal, there is a sculpture under the altar
that shows Peter sleeping. In fact, this is exactly what happened.
Jesus asked Peter, James, and John to watch while he prayed,
but they fell asleep. "And he came and found them sleeping,
and he said to Peter, 'Simon, are you asleep? Could you not
watch one hour? Watch and pray that you may not enter
into temptation; the spirit indeed is willing, but the flesh is
weak'" (Mk 14:37–38). Notice that all three of the Apostles fell
asleep, but it was Peter who bore the brunt of the reprimand.
It's similar to when parents come home and find all of their
children misbehaving. While they've all misbehaved equally,
it's usually the oldest one who gets the tongue lashing and the
punishment because more is expected from him or her. Here,
Jesus expects Peter to be the most responsible. He's the first of
the Twelve, in a sense the oldest. Twice more Jesus went off to
pray, yet twice more he returned to find his disciples asleep.
The third time he told them, "It is enough; the hour has come;
the Son of man is betrayed into the hands of sinners. Rise, let
us be going; see, my betrayer is at hand" (Mk 14:41–42).

Christ's words "to watch and pray" are highly significant.
God gave the ordinance to Moses that the Passover was to
be a night of vigil and watching for all generations. Recall

the first Passover meal in Egypt. The Israelites ate the meal, but then waited and prayed because they knew the angel of death would be coming. In imitation of that first vigil, Moses instructed the Israelites that they should keep this annual vigil for all generations. Here in the Gospel, we see Jesus celebrate the Passover by watching and praying.

What time would it have been at the "hour" of Jesus's arrest? Working backwards, we know that the Last Supper would have taken place from about six until nine at night, at which time Jesus went with his disciples to the Garden of Gethsemane. The Gospel tells us that Jesus prayed for three hours, returning each hour to check on Peter, James, and John. Thus, after the third time returning to the sleeping trio, it would have been around midnight. What does Jesus say? "The hour has come." The Book of Exodus tells us that the angel of death came at midnight in the original Passover (*cf.* Ex 11:4). By comparison, Judas is the new angel of death who, like the first, also comes at midnight—but unlike the first, he is sent not by God but by Satan.

Extending this comparison, we read in the Old Testament that lambs were sacrificed at the first Passover so that the first-born sons would be spared. However, when we read the story of the Last Supper in the New Testament, there is no mention of a lamb. This is because the Passover lamb was a substitute for the sacrifice. In this case, there will be no substitute. Jesus himself is the sacrificial lamb—the first-born Son who will be sacrificed—and so there is no lamb mentioned at the Last Supper.

Jesus's Arrest and Peter's Betrayal

Judas arrived in the Garden of Gethsemane at midnight with the soldiers who would arrest Jesus. Luke's account of this episode tells us,

> While [Jesus] was still speaking, there came a crowd, and the man called Judas, one of the Twelve, was leading them. He drew near to Jesus to kiss him; but Jesus said to him, "Judas, would you betray the Son of man with a kiss?" And when those who were about him saw what would follow, they said, "Lord, shall we strike with the sword?" And one of them struck the slave of the high priest and cut off his right ear. But Jesus said, "No more of this!" And he touched his ear and healed him. (Lk 22:47–48)

Of course, we know who it was who struck out with the sword—Peter.

> Then Jesus said to the chief priests and captains of the temple and elders, who had come out against him, "Have you come out as against a robber, with swords and clubs? When I was with you day after day in the temple, you did not lay hands on me. But this is your hour, and the power of darkness." Then they seized him and led him away, bringing him into the high priest's house. (Lk 22:52–54)

The Gospel tells us that "Peter followed at a distance" (Lk 22:54). This phrase, "followed at a distance," is a haunting verse in Luke's account of the Passion, as we shall see. The soldiers took Jesus to Caiaphas's house across the Kidron Valley. There was a staircase that went right past Caiaphas's house on a road down to the Kidron Valley. Those steps have been excavated, so you can see the very steps that Jesus walked on. The irony is that further up from Caiaphas's house is the Zion quarter of Jerusalem where Jesus celebrated the Last Supper. So Jesus went down those very stairs with the Twelve following the Passover meal as they made their way toward the Garden of Gethsemane. Following his arrest, Jesus retraced his steps, led by a very different escort, who took him up these same steps to Caiaphas's house. Today, the Church of St. Peter Gallicantu stands upon the archaeological ruins of what was Caiaphas's house, located just outside the Old City of Jerusalem. *Gallicantu* is Latin for "rooster," or cock, and a rooster is going to play a key role in what happens next.

Luke's Gospel sets the stage for the events that follow Jesus's arrest by saying, "Peter followed at a distance; and when they had kindled a fire in the middle of the courtyard and sat down together, Peter sat among them" (Lk 22:54–55). It's early spring, so it still would have been cold at night. That's why the disciples probably spent the night in a cave, where it would have been warmer. Here, Peter was cold and wanted to warm himself by the fire. "Then a maid, seeing him as he sat in the light and gazing at him, said, 'This man also was with him'" (Lk 22:56). In the Gospels, discipleship is defined as being with Jesus. Therefore, it is highly significant that the maid uses the past tense, "This man also *was* with him," which indicates that Peter was no longer with Christ.

As bad as this might seem for Peter's faithfulness, it is paltry compared with what happens next. "But he denied [that he was with Jesus], saying, 'Woman, I do not know him.' And a little later some one else saw him and said, 'You also are one of them.' But Peter said, 'Man, I am not.' And after an interval of about an hour still another insisted, saying, 'Certainly this man also was with him; for he is a Galilean'" (Lk 22:57–59). Fellow Jews immediately could tell from his accent that Peter was from Galilee, just like an American can tell when someone is from, say, the Deep South or New England. When questioned a third time Peter replied, "'Man, I do not know what you are saying.' And immediately, while he was still speaking, the

Icon of Peter's threefold denial in
St. Peter Gallicantu, Jerusalem

cock crowed. And the Lord turned and looked at Peter. And Peter remembered the word of the Lord, how he had said to him, 'Before the cock crows today, you will deny me three times.' And he went out and wept bitterly" (Lk 22:60–62).

It was in the courtyard of Caiaphas, just outside the Church of St. Peter Gallicantu, that Peter thrice betrayed Christ. Inside the church there is a beautiful icon that illustrates this gospel episode quite well. The icon presents several scenes at once. In the background, you see Peter and the maid exchanging words on either side of a fire. Peter is wearing a gold robe and gesturing with his hands that he doesn't know Christ. Elevated on a column in the center of the icon is the rooster—the *gallicantu*. And in the foreground you see two figures standing side by side, but not too close: Christ looking at Peter after his thrice betrayal. It's a striking contrast that while Peter's hands are gesturing denial and almost pushing Jesus away, Jesus's hands are bound. He's a prisoner.

In the center of the sanctuary, behind the altar in the lower church, there's another icon that shows us what happens after: Peter weeping bitterly. I love the Latin Vulgate translation of this verse, posted on a plaque beside the icon: "*Et egressus foras Petrus flevit amare.*" In English, this verse is normally translated "And [Peter] went out and wept bitterly" (Lk 22:62). This bitterness with which Peter wept isn't just any ordinary bitterness. Rather, it is the bitterness of one utterly sorrowful for having betrayed his beloved. Peter fled and wept for love because the one he betrayed is love incarnate.

This is a powerful moment for Peter. Interestingly, the icon places the weeping Peter in the Cave of Betrayal. Peter is shown as having fled to the place he would go so often to be with Jesus and to hear him teach.

Icon of Peter weeping in St. Peter Gallicantu, Jerusalem

Considering Peter's betrayal of Jesus, we can see that it was preceded by his following Jesus "from a distance." If we follow Christ in a discipleship that is comfortable and easy—from a distance—we're setting ourselves up for a discipleship that will end in denial. You can't follow at a distance and remain a disciple for very long—a true one, at least. Have you ever tried to follow someone in a car when you don't know the directions or where they are going? If you get separated because they go too fast or you have to stop at a light, then you are lost. To prevent this, you have to follow the car as closely as possible. It's the same way with Christ. Following at a distance might seem comfortable and easy at first, but eventually we get separated from Christ, and then we're lost.

Like Peter, the question for us is whether we are following Christ from a distance. Is that the key description of our discipleship? It's easy to fall into the trap of thinking we're a disciple of Jesus and doing well so long as we don't do all of the bad things that we see in the world. But after a while we begin to put our discipleship on the back-burner. We get busy with our own lives and our own plans. But remember, it's not about our will. Jesus shows us this clearly in the Garden of Gethsemane when he says, "Father, if you are willing, remove this chalice from me; nevertheless not my will, but yours, be done" (Lk 22:42). This is the discipleship of a Son who is close to his Father. In essence, Jesus models in a positive way how we should follow God closely, while Peter models in a negative way how we should not follow from a distance. As we move through the Passion narrative, Peter poignantly illustrates the question of discipleship. Are we following Jesus at a distance? This is dangerous because—as was the case with Peter—it can lead to denial. And we can't be certain that, also like Peter, we will have the courage and conviction to repent and go on to become saints.

"Now the men who were holding Jesus mocked him and beat him; they also blindfolded him and asked him, 'Prophesy! Who is it that struck you?'" (Lk 22:63–64). There is a great paradox in these verses. As the soldiers mocked Jesus as a prophet and commanded him to prophesy, Christ's prophecy made during the Last Supper was fulfilled: outside in the courtyard, Peter denied even knowing the Lord three times.

If we didn't know the end of the story, Peter's denial of Christ at this point in the Gospel might make us question what kind of leader he was going to make. Perhaps Jesus made a mistake in choosing him. But we know that Peter would make a great leader because of his repentance and experience of God's mercy. Forgiveness is the main theme that will punctuate Peter's preaching. We will see this over and over in the Acts of the Apostles and in Peter's New Testament epistles. Peter understands perfectly that it is in Christ that we find forgiveness of sins. He is the best expositor of that truth because he is the first recipient of Christ's forgiveness after the Resurrection.

Ironically, God can use our failures for our own discipleship. This is an astonishing truth. No matter what our sins might be, God can use our sinful past for his praise and glory. Just think for a moment of people who have made tremendous mistakes in their life and have so much regret. Yet, through repentance, they can receive God's forgiveness and turn that regret into a beacon of God's mercy, becoming a witness of God's love. Whatever Satan does to tear us down, God can use to build us up in the truth of his mercy, love, and glory. I always think of sinners like Peter who betrayed the Lord, and now give eternal glory to God because they became signs of God's great mercy and forgiveness. That's what repentant sinners do for all eternity, and Peter is the foremost example.

Peter's Threefold Affirmation

In the Church of St. Peter Gallicantu, there is a third icon to the right of the altar that depicts a scene from the Gospel of John. Following the Resurrection, Jesus tells the disciples to meet him in Galilee. Peter goes up to Galilee with the others and starts fishing again. "Just as day was breaking, Jesus stood on the beach; yet the disciples did not know that it was Jesus" (Jn 21:4). Remember the theme of waiting on God more than the watchman waits for dawn from Psalm 130 and Isaiah. Here we have Jesus appearing to the disciples at dawn.

"Jesus said to them, 'Children, have you any fish?' They answered him, 'No.' He said to them, 'Cast the net on the right side of the boat, and you will find some.' So they cast it, and now they were not able to haul it in, for the quantity of fish" (Jn 21:5–6). There is no fish on one side of the boat, yet on the other side there are so many fish that they can't even haul in the net. "That disciple whom Jesus loved said to Peter, 'It is the Lord!' When Simon Peter heard that it was the Lord, he put on his clothes, for he was stripped for work, and sprang into the sea" (Jn 21:7). Peter had been in the water working the nets and so had removed his clothes to avoid getting them wet. Now he puts his clothes back on and immediately jumps into the water. "But the other disciples came in the boat, dragging the net full of fish, for they were not far from the land, but about a hundred yards off. When they got out on land, they saw a charcoal fire there, with fish lying on it, and bread" (Jn 21:8–9). We only find a charcoal fire mentioned twice in the Gospels. We first encountered one in John 18:18, when Peter denied Jesus three times, and here we see it again. We'll see there is a close relationship between these two occurrences.

> When they had finished breakfast, Jesus said to Simon Peter, "Simon, son of John, do you love me more than these?" He said to him, "Yes, Lord; you know that I love you." He said to him, "Feed my lambs." A second time he said to him, "Simon, son of John, do you love me?" He said to him, "Yes, Lord; you know that I love you." He said to him, "Tend my sheep." He said to him the third time, "Simon, son of John, do you love me?" Peter was grieved because he said to him the third time, "Do you love me?" And he said to him, "Lord, you know everything; you know that I love you." Jesus said to him, "Feed my sheep." (Jn 21:15–17)

Peter was grieved because Jesus asked him a third time whether he loved him. Why is this third time important, and why was Peter grieved? It's because he suddenly understood the significance of Jesus's third question. The last time that he was at a charcoal fire, Peter had denied Christ three times. Now, Christ asks him three times if he loves him. Jesus isn't rubbing it in; rather, Jesus is giving him a chance to affirm his love—to undo his threefold denial. This is beautifully illustrated in the icon at St. Peter Gallicantu. The icon on the right, which depicts Peter's threefold affirmation of love, brings to completion the icon on the left, which depicts Peter's threefold denial. The center icon, Peter's repentance as he weeps in the cave, makes possible his threefold affirmation.

Again, it's interesting to look at Peter's hands. Whereas before, his hands were gesturing his threefold denial of Christ, now his hands are held out toward the Lord to receive the shepherd's staff ("Feed my lambs," "tend my sheep"). Peter accepts this mission to be the Church's shepherd. As Jesus taught early in the Gospel of John, the good shepherd lays down his life for his sheep. It's not just about power and authority; it means responsibility and self-sacrificial love.

Icon of Peter's threefold affirmation in
St. Peter Gallicantu, Jerusalem

By giving him the shepherd's staff, the icon indicates that Peter's denial did not negate his role in Jesus's mission and plan. This is a beautiful way to bring the story together. It highlights the prominence of Peter and his witness to Jesus's love, mercy, and forgiveness. We'll see this theme of mercy and forgiveness continue in the Acts of the Apostles.

Peter and the Rooster

One of the great images associated with Peter in Christian art is the rooster. In many early Christian sarcophagi in the catacombs, you will see a rooster placed right in front of Peter. This is evidence that from the earliest years, the rooster was the dominant image associated with Peter. This is especially emphasized in the Church of St. Peter Gallicantu, which has a large golden rooster on top of the church. Let's take a moment to examine an ancient Christian poem about the rooster, "On the Wings of the Dawn." It was composed by a pilgrim called Prudentius, who traveled to Jerusalem from Spain around AD 400. The Church adopted this poem for Tuesday morning prayer (lauds) in the old Roman Breviary, where it is known as *Ales diei nuntius*, "Winged Herald of the Day." In Roman art, the image of the rooster represented the herald of the dawn. Because of this, it naturally became associated with Peter who betrayed Our Lord before dawn and also, after the Resurrection, professed his love for Christ before dawn.

Because of this episode with Peter following the Resurrection, the rooster became a sign of the resurrected Lord, who reaffirmed Peter's call to be the shepherd of his sheep. So this is what Prudentius wrote, and what the Church traditionally sung every Tuesday morning:

> The winged herald of the day
> Proclaims the morn's approaching ray:
> So Christ the Lord renews his call,

This comes from John 21, when Jesus called Peter to "feed my lambs ... tend my sheep ... feed my sheep."

> To endless life awakening all.
> "Take up thy bed," to each he cries,
> Who sick or wrapped in slumber lies:
> "Be chaste and living soberly,
> Watch ye, for I the lord am nigh."

Like the paralytic who takes up his bed and rises, Christ is calling us who slumber to wake up and rise.

> With earnest cry, with tearful care,
> Call we the Lord to hear our prayer;
> While supplication pure and deep,
> Forbids each chastened heart to sleep.

In these verses, sleep is a metaphor that signifies spiritual sleep in contrast to being awake and seeing the light. When you are sleeping you remain in the dark, but when you awake you come into the light. This same theme is used by Paul in his one of his epistles when he says, "Awake, O sleeper, and arise from the dead, and Christ shall give you light" (Eph 5:14). What did Peter do in the Passion narrative? Instead of watching, waiting, and praying, he fell asleep in the garden. He ended up living discipleship at a distance, which eventually led him to deny Christ. If Peter could have stayed awake and kept vigil, he would have found the grace to remain faithful to Christ. And so this hymn of the Church, which used to be prayed early every Tuesday morning throughout the world, calls us to rise with the dawn and to be vigilant in prayer.

> O Father, that we ask be done,
> Through Jesus Christ, thine only son;
> Who, with the Holy Ghost and thee,
> Shall live and reign eternally.

What a beautiful hymn of the dawn to awaken us from sleep. Though it never mentions Peter by name, the mention of the rooster and awaking the dawn are clear allusions to the story of Peter. This imagery of Peter and the dawn is a great way for us to end this chapter. Peter fell asleep, he fell at a distance, and he fell when he denied Christ, but then he was forgiven at the dawn of the Resurrection by the infinite mercy of God—and then given the admonition to shepherd Christ's sheep. Peter will be a great shepherd because he can speak from the heart about the forgiveness that can be found in Christ. This makes Peter the model disciple. We are to witness to the world just as Peter did—not by condemning the world but by proclaiming that we are sinners who have found forgiveness in Christ. We have found the mercy of God the Father and the love of Jesus Christ. By his Resurrection, he has freed us. This is the good news that we are called to share with the world. May we, like Peter, proclaim God's mercy and forgiveness to a world that lives in darkness. May we awake—and may we awake many others—to the dawn of God's light, mercy, and love.

Chapter 8

Peter and Pentecost: The Transforming Power of the Holy Spirit

In the last chapter, we studied the story of Peter from the beginning of the Passion narrative through the Resurrection of Christ. We saw how the rooster—the *gallicantu*—became the iconic symbol for Peter in the early Church. The rooster represents the great watchman of dawn, which reminds us not only of Peter's threefold denial of Christ but also of his threefold affirmation. It also reminds us of the summons that Christ gives Peter to care for his sheep.

We will turn now to the story of the early Church, which is found in the Acts of the Apostles. While the book's title suggests that it's about the acts of all twelve Apostles, it focuses primarily on two of them—Peter, who will be the dominant figure in the first half of the book, and Paul in the second.

Noble Deeds

An examination of the genre of the Acts of the Apostles is very revealing. The Greek word for "acts" is *praxis*, which means "deeds" or "actions." The term *praxis*, however, as used in the ancient world, normally referred to the actions of a great man. Although this literary genre became popular in the first century, it actually goes back to Aristotle, the great Greek philosopher who wrote books on physics, philosophy, ethics, as well as many other subjects. Aristotle categorized all things so as to abstract principles from them that he believed would give wisdom. Whether it was principles on law, ethics, or virtue, he sought to formulate ideas about human behavior that would help build good character and assist us in living our lives well. But when he looked at history, Aristotle came to believe that most wisdom that could be abstracted from a subject wasn't universal but particular, often turning on what seem to be accidents in human affairs. For example, the outcome of a battle might depend on such chance factors as weather conditions or a particular person having happened to be on the field. However, the one thing that Aristotle believed could be learned from history was how the deeds of great men help to build the *polis*, the Greek term for "city." So, viewed in this light, *praxis* referred to the noble deeds of great men who built the *polis*. Since, for the Greeks and Romans, culture and civilization could only be found in the city, the term *polis* became synonymous with what today we would refer to as civilization.

This is the backdrop of the literary genre that was dedicated to studying the *praxis* or actions of great men so as to better understand how to build a civilization. While there were many classic works in the Latin and Greek periods, the *Praxis* or *Acts of Caesar Augustus* came to epitomize this entire genre. The book was commissioned by Augustus to be published all over the Roman Empire in both Greek and Latin so that everyone could come to know what a great man he was and how blessed the world was to have him and the Roman Empire that he helped build. Augustus listed all of the noble deeds that he had performed to build up the common good and initiate the *pax Romana*. His aim was pedagogical: to teach the barbarian tribes Rome conquered and the peoples it had subjugated why Roman rule was beneficial for them, and why it was for their own good to submit to Caesar and give him homage.

Luke—the most Greek-minded of the New Testament writers—had his finger on the pulse of the Greco-Roman culture of the time, and so decided to write the story of the early Church using this literary genre. In a sense, Luke was subverting the Greek and Roman *praxis* stories by showing that the Apostles were the ones building a new civilization—the new Rome. Luke, in a way, is telling us that if we're going to build the New Jerusalem, as it was called by St. Paul, or the City of God, as it was later called by St. Augustine, we need to look to the Apostles as models.

With this idea of the *praxis* genre in mind, we'll take a detailed look at how the Apostles lived and the community they built. In doing so, we'll study four key marks of the early Christian community. The first mark of the early Christians is that they *listened* to the teachings of the Apostles who were setting the stage for this new way of life. These were the "great men" who were building up this great culture and civilization.

The Ascension and the Promise of the Holy Spirit

The Acts of the Apostles begins with the Ascension of Jesus into Heaven. Luke's Gospel places the disciples on the Mount of Olives when they witnessed this event. This is significant when viewed in the light of another ascension found in the Old Testament. In the Second Book of Kings, we read about Elijah ascending into Heaven. Before this happened, Elisha asked Elijah for a double portion of his spirit. This was a tremendous request, so Elijah answered, "You have asked a hard thing; yet, if you see me as I am being taken from you, it shall be so for you; but if you do not see me, it shall not be so" (2 Kgs 2:10). Then Elisha saw Elijah taken up in a fiery chariot. As was promised, Elisha received a double portion of his spirit and performed twice as many miracles as Elijah.

The fact that the Book of Acts begins with the disciples witnessing Christ's Ascension means that, like Elisha, we can expect them to receive a double portion of his spirit—the Holy Spirit. And this is exactly what happens at Pentecost, which we'll read about in the second chapter of Acts. By starting with the Ascension, Luke is showing us how that event leads directly to Pentecost. It is the Ascension that leads to the gift of the Holy Spirit at Pentecost—and Peter will say this explicitly in his Pentecost homily. While these two feasts are close together in time, occurring only ten days apart, we often don't connect them as much as we should.

His Office Let Another Take

After the Ascension, Luke records, the Apostles returned to Jerusalem, "and when they had entered, they went up to the upper room, where they were staying, Peter and John and James and Andrew, Philip and Thomas, Bartholomew and Matthew, James the son of Alphae'us and Simon the Zealot and Judas the son of James" (Acts 1:12). There were two named Judas among the Twelve Apostles—Judas Iscariot, who betrayed Christ, and Judas, the son of James. Notice that Judas Iscariot is not present.

At this point in the Acts of the Apostles, we begin to see Peter taking on the leadership position in the early Church. For example, when we look at the list of the Apostles who were present, we see that Luke names Peter first. While this was the case in the Gospels, this particular instance is significant as it is the first time that the Apostles are listed following the Ascension. By placing Peter first, Luke is emphasizing his leadership role. Peter is the prime minister, the *ha al bayyit*.

"All these with one accord devoted themselves to prayer, together with the women and Mary the mother of Jesus, and with his brethren" (Acts 1:14). Notice that Luke gives Mary special mention.

> In those days Peter stood up among the brethren (the company of persons was in all about a hundred and twenty), and said, "Brethren, the Scripture had to be fulfilled, which the Holy Spirit spoke beforehand by the mouth of David, concerning Judas who was guide to those who arrested Jesus. For he was numbered among us, and was allotted his share in this ministry." (Acts 1:15–17)

It is important that Peter said Judas was "allotted" a share in Christ's ministry, and that they were going to cast "lots" to replace him. A few verses later, Peter explained: "For it is written in the book of Psalms, 'Let his habitation become desolate, and let there be no one to live in it'; and 'His office let another take'" (Acts 1:20). Remember how Shebna, the prime minister in Israel, was replaced by Eliakim in the Book of Isaiah. Now, the same thing is happening here. The position Judas had vacated by his suicide was to be filled by someone who would take his office and exercise his authority. This is important because it indicates that the Twelve Apostles weren't just friends or followers of Jesus, but rather they had been appointed by Christ to rule over his kingdom. Just as there were the Twelve Tribes of Israel, there were Twelve Apostles who held twelve offices in the new kingdom. They had authority given by Jesus. We see this clearly in Luke's Gospel when, before celebrating the Last Supper, Jesus said, "As my Father appointed a kingdom for me, so do I appoint for you that you may eat and drink at my table in my kingdom, and sit on thrones judging the twelve tribes of Israel" (Lk 22:29–30). At the beginning of Acts, we see that this appointment signifies that the Twelve held an actual office. They weren't merely twelve disciples who happened to be especially close to Christ and were called Apostles on this account alone.

Peter then gave the qualifications for the person who would take Judas's office. He would have to be "one of the men who have accompanied us during all the time that the Lord Jesus went in and out among us, beginning from the baptism of John until the day when he was taken up from us—one of these men must become with us a witness to his resurrection" (Acts 1:21–22). An Apostle must be someone who witnessed the Resurrection because the Resurrection is the defining moment that changed everything.

"And they put forward two, Joseph called Barsab'bas, who was surnamed Justus, and Matthi'as. And they prayed and said, 'Lord, you know the hearts of all men, show which one of these two you have chosen to take the place in this ministry and apostleship from which Judas turned aside, to go to his own place'" (Acts 1:23–25). "To go to his own place" is a euphemism for what really happened to Judas. "And they cast lots for them, and the lot fell on Matthi'as; and he was enrolled with the eleven apostles" (Acts 1:26). We see that there were two qualified candidates and so the question arose of which to choose and how to choose him. Peter was in charge, and he had a decision to make, and he decided they should cast lots.

This used to strike me as strange, as though Peter couldn't make up his mind. It seemed to me as if the pressure of leadership and the need to make the tough decisions had already proven too much for him. However, the practice of casting lots goes back to the traditions of Israel. In First Chronicles, we read that David established Jerusalem as the permanent location for the Temple and appointed the Levite priests to minister in the Temple. There were many different priestly duties, such as preparing the animal sacrifices and taking care of the altar of incense. So, to prevent disagreements and abuses when it came time for a Levite to minister in the Temple, it was provided that lots should be cast to decide which tasks each of the priests should perform.

First Chronicles tells us,

> With the help of Za'dok of the sons of Elea'zar, and Ahim'elech
> of the sons of Ith'amar, David organized them according to the
> appointed duties in their service. Since more chief men were found
> among the sons of Elea'zar than among the sons of Ith'amar, they
> organized them under sixteen heads of fathers' houses of the sons
> of Elea'zar, and eight of the sons of Ith'amar. They organized them
> by lot, all alike, for there were officers of the sanctuary and officers
> of God among both the sons of Elea'zar and the sons of Itha'mar.
> And the scribe Shemai'ah the son of Nethan'el, a Levite, recorded
> them in the presence of the king, and the princes, and Za'dok the
> priest, and Ahim'elech the son of Abi'athar, and the heads of the
> fathers' houses of the priests and of the Levites; one father's house
> being chosen for Elea'zar and one chosen for Ith'amar.... These
> also, the head of each father's house and his younger brother alike,
> cast lots, just as their brethren the sons of Aaron, in the presence of
> King David, Za'dok, Ahim'elech, and the heads of fathers' houses
> of the priests and of the Levites. (1 Chr 24:3–6, 31)

So lots were cast to determine which priestly job the men
of the Tribe of Levi would be assigned. Notice that the lots
were cast and recorded in the presence of the king. We also
see evidence of this practice of casting lots in Luke's Gospel,
when Zechariah was chosen by lots to go to the altar of
incense (*cf.* Lk 1:9). This was the most important task that
could be given to a Levite priest, and Zechariah had never
been assigned this job before.

Following this Old Testament precedent, Peter cast lots
to determine who would take Judas's office. This "casting

of lots" tells us a couple of very important things. First, the office held by the Apostles was a priestly office. Secondly, Peter was overseeing the casting of lots, just as David did in the Old Testament. Jesus is the king, the New David, but he has ascended into Heaven. So, Peter steps in as the *ha al bayyit*, the "prime minister." This is a small detail, but it's infused with meaning when you understand the biblical history of Israel, and it reinforces Peter's leadership position among the Apostles.

Pentecost and God's Glory

After Matthias's election, the next thing that we read in Acts is that the Feast of Pentecost had arrived. While we normally think of Pentecost in relation to the Holy Spirit, it is important to remember that this was a Jewish feast—one of the three major ones—which celebrated the first harvest.

> When the day of Pentecost had come, they were all together in one place. And suddenly a sound came from heaven like the rush of a mighty wind, and it filled all the house where they were sitting. And there appeared to them tongues as of fire, distributed and resting on each one of them. And they were all filled with the Holy Spirit and began to speak in other tongues, as the Spirit gave them utterance. (Acts 2:1–4)

It is commonly assumed that the descent of the Holy Spirit in the Pentecost story took place in the Upper Room. However, Luke never tells us this. He mentions the Upper Room in the first chapter of Acts, but here he simply says that they were gathered together in one place. As pious Jews, they would have been celebrating the Feast of Pentecost in the Temple. Although Luke does not specify this in Acts, I would propose that they were gathered in the Temple. This makes more sense when you consider the great crowd that is mentioned in the next verse. "Now there were dwelling in Jerusalem Jews, devout men from every nation under heaven. And at this sound the multitude came together, and they were bewildered, because each one heard them speaking in his own language" (Acts 2:5–6). Because this was a major pilgrimage feast, large numbers of Jews and God-fearers— Gentiles who were sympathetic to Judaism—would make a pilgrimage to Jerusalem. The great multitude, which came together from many nations, were bewildered because they heard the Apostles speaking in their own languages.

> And they were amazed and wondered, saying, "Are not all these who are speaking Galileans? And how is it that we hear, each of us in his own native language? ... we hear them telling in our own tongues the mighty works of God." And all were amazed and perplexed, saying to one another, "What does this mean?" But others mocking said, "They are filled with new wine." But Peter, standing with the Eleven, lifted up his voice and addressed them, "Men of Judea and all who dwell in Jerusalem, let this be known to you, and give ear to my words. For these men are not drunk, as you suppose, since it is only the third hour of the day." (Acts 2:7–8, 11–15)

If the disciples were still in the Upper Room, then how could the people have heard them speaking? Later, we are told that the number who believed and were baptized were over three thousand. Again, the Baptism of three thousand people couldn't have taken place in the Upper Room. This great number could have been accommodated, however, if the theory is correct that they were gathered in the Temple.

In light of Jewish history, it is significant if the Holy Spirit descended upon the disciples in the Temple. When Solomon finished building the first Temple and dedicated it, the glory of the Lord—the *Shekinah* or "the glory cloud," with the spirit of God—came down and descended on the Temple. This great event visibly manifested God's spirit in the Temple. A similar thing happened in the desert with the Tabernacle that housed the Ark of the Covenant. After they built the Tabernacle and attended a meeting, the glory cloud of the Lord came down and overshadowed the Tabernacle and filled it with God's presence. However, Solomon's Temple had been destroyed, and the Jews sent into exile. Upon their return, they rebuilt the Temple, albeit on a much humbler scale, but God's glory had not returned.

Later, when Herod the Great began his massive rebuilding of the Temple, there was an expectation that God's glory would finally come back to the Temple. At this time, Israel would be vindicated from her enemies and the age of the Messiah would be inaugurated. Herod began this great rebuilding of the Temple in 18 BC, but it wouldn't be finished until AD 66. Thus, construction was still ongoing at the time of this first Christian Pentecost. Unfortunately, as soon as the Temple was complete, Israel declared war against Rome, and the Romans destroyed the Temple merely four years after its completion.

The irony is that God wasn't waiting for the Jews to finish rebuilding the Temple. Here, on the Feast of Pentecost, he sent the Holy Spirit. Jesus had prepared the way for this great event through his Death on the Cross, his glorious Resurrection, and his Ascension into Heaven. From the right hand of the Father, he intercedes for us. He atoned for Israel's sins—and ours—and promised to ask the Father to send the Holy Spirit. God was not waiting for the Jerusalem Temple to be finished; rather, he was waiting for the greater work of the true temple—Jesus's Body—to be completed. This is what inaugurated Pentecost.

We can see this relationship between Christ's Body and the Temple in the beginning of John's Gospel when Jesus said, "Destroy this temple, and in three days I will raise it up" (Jn 2:19). The temple of Christ's Body is complete in the Resurrection, and once he ascended into Heaven, the glory of the Lord could come back to Israel. So, presuming the theory is correct, here at Pentecost God brought the Spirit back to the Temple as he foretold in Ezekiel (*cf.* Ez 43).

Peter, preaching to the gathered crowd, quoted the prophet Joel, who foretold: "And in the last days it shall be, God declares, that I will pour out my Spirit upon all flesh" (Acts 2:17). Peter was saying that what had just happened at Pentecost—the Spirit of God being poured out—fulfilled the prophets.

The New David

The humble fisherman, now filled with the Holy Spirit, continued preaching boldly to his fellow Jews:

> "Men of Israel, hear these words: Jesus of Nazareth, a man attested to you by God with mighty works and wonders and signs which God did through him in your midst, as you yourselves know—this Jesus,

delivered up according to the definite plan and foreknowledge of God, you crucified and killed by the hands of lawless men. But God raised him up, having loosed the pangs of death, because it was not possible for him to be held by it." (Acts 2:22–24)

Peter then quoted Psalm 16 to show how the Resurrection was central to the Davidic plan and to the Davidic house, and, by extension, to all of Israel. "For David says concerning him, 'I saw the Lord always before me, for he is at my right hand that I may not be shaken; therefore my heart was glad, and my tongue rejoiced; moreover my flesh will dwell in hope'" (Acts 2:25–26). In order to help his listeners understand Jesus, Peter took them back to David because he knew that Jesus is the Christ, the Anointed One, the New David. Peter was the first to understand this. Peter quoted David, speaking about Jesus Christ so many centuries before (*cf.* Ps 16:10): "For you will not abandon my [David's] soul to Hades, nor let your Holy One see corruption. You have made known to me the ways of life; you will make me full of gladness with your presence" (Acts 2:27–28).

Here is the promise that the Holy One will not see corruption. Although this is a Psalm of David, it can't apply to David since his body wasn't incorrupt. "Brethren, I may say to you confidently of the patriarch David that he both died and was buried, and his tomb is with us to this day" (Act 2:29). All the Jews knew where David was buried, so how could the Psalm say that he would not see corruption and that his soul would not go to Hades? While that may seem problematic in terms of the fulfillment of the Psalm, Peter offered the answer.

The answer is that David was speaking prophetically about the New David, the Messiah. "Being therefore a prophet, and knowing that God had sworn with an oath to him that he would set one of his descendants upon his throne, he foresaw and spoke of the resurrection of the Christ, that he was not abandoned to Hades, nor did his flesh see corruption" (Acts 2:30–31). Peter's words here come from Second Samuel where God promised David that one of his descendants would be established on a throne forever and his kingdom would never end. Jesus is this promised heir of David, whose kingdom will last forever. Jesus suffered death, but his soul wasn't abandoned to Hades. Not only was he victorious over death but he brought the souls of the just out of Hades. In this way, Jesus's Resurrection fulfilled the promise of David in Psalm 16.

The Power of a Witness

Peter was a constant witness to the great saving deeds of Jesus and stressed their importance.

> "This Jesus God raised up, and of that we all are witnesses. Being therefore exalted at the right hand of God, and having received from the Father the promise of the Holy Spirit, he has poured out this which you see and hear. For David did not ascend into the heavens; but he himself says, 'The Lord said to my Lord, Sit at my right hand, till I make your enemies a stool for your feet.' Let all the house of Israel therefore know assuredly that God has made him both Lord and Christ, this Jesus whom you crucified." (Acts 2:32–36)

Peter often talked about being a witness. We see this theme in his preaching throughout the Book of Acts and in his epistles. This is important for us in our study of the Faith. As Peter wrote, "Always be prepared to make a defense to any one who calls you to account for the hope that is in you" (1 Pt 3:15). We aren't so much going to win others by brilliant argument. In fact, our first and foremost role is not to be catechists (teachers of the Faith) to the world. We primarily catechize those who are already in the Church. When it comes to the world, our role is not that of a teacher to a student, but rather to be a witness. In a sense, there is a great trial that the world has to constantly face. The accuser, Satan, is the prosecuting attorney who is constantly attacking God, his plan, and his Church. The followers of Christ, on the other hand, are witnesses for the defense who testify to Jesus's holiness, his purity, his goodness, and most importantly his Resurrection. Thus, the role of the Church, as Peter outlined here, is to be a witness. I think this idea of being a witness is vital to our studies of Peter. Sometimes we may wish that we could have a Bible scholar explain everything to the people we want to convert, but that's not the point. The world isn't ready for long lectures on the Faith. Rather, the world needs witnesses.

Knowing Christ radically changes our lives and gives us a peace and joy that we never had before. It makes us free of anxiety and free to be receptive to others and to respond to their needs. We are called to be a witness to the joy of Christ and to the peace that comes from knowing him. We are witnesses to the world that forgiveness, love, and mercy come from knowing and loving Christ. We share these truths with others when we show the difference that Jesus makes in our lives. Since the Gospel does this for us, it's essential to remember that the first part of evangelization is simply to be a witness to Christ. This makes our job considerably easier. As Paul says, not all are called to be teachers, but we can all be witnesses. Witnessing to the Faith is much more effective than, say, an exposition of Bible passages according to the original Greek and Hebrew because witnessing is much more authentic and from the heart. This was beautifully illustrated by Peter when he appeared before the Jewish authorities. The scribes and Pharisees viewed Peter as uneducated, but he made an extremely effective witness. Like Peter, each of us is called by God to be a witness not just by our words but by our attitudes and actions.

At Pentecost, three thousand souls came to believe and be baptized. That is how effective this type of evangelization really is. Peter wasn't an educated man; he simply witnessed his own experience of Jesus and what he knew. We should not be afraid or let the little we know prevent us from being witnesses, too.

Repentance and Baptism

Peter continued his homily by calling the crowd to repentance. "Now when they heard this they were cut to the heart, and said to Peter and the rest of the apostles, 'Brethren, what shall we do?' And Peter said to them, 'Repent, and be baptized every one of you in the name of Jesus Christ for the forgiveness of your sins; and you shall receive the gift of the Holy

Spirit'" (Acts 2:37–38). Peter could preach powerfully about God's forgiveness because he had experienced it first-hand.

"'For the promise is to you and to your children and to all that are far off, every one whom the Lord our God calls to him.' And he testified with many other words and exhorted them, saying, 'Save yourselves from this crooked generation.' So those who received his word were baptized, and there were added that day about three thousand souls" (Acts 2:39–41). The promise that Peter was referring to is the gift of the Holy Spirit that he spoke about earlier in verse thirty-three. What is the condition for receiving the gift of the Holy Spirit? Repentance and being baptized for the forgiveness of sins. This brings us back to our earlier study of Capernaum, the "village of consolation." Peter unveiled the promise of the Holy Spirit, which was for them and their children, and told them to save themselves from this "crooked generation." The people were cut to the heart and realized the tragedy of their separation from God. They desired this Baptism that would bring them the gift of the Paraclete, the consoler. Baptism is the key, and three thousand were baptized that very day.

Where could the Apostles have baptized three thousand people? There wouldn't have been enough space in the Upper Room. Again, I would propose that this was done outside of the Temple. When you visit Jerusalem, you can see some of the remaining steps that would have formed the southern entrance to the Temple. These would have been the actual steps that pilgrims such as Jesus, Peter, John, and our Blessed Mother would have climbed as they went up to the gates of the Temple. At the bottom of these steps, and to the right of the Temple, were a group of *mikvaot,* ritual bathing places. Before entering the Temple, pilgrims would have a ritual bath of purification. These baths have been excavated so you can get a good idea of how this was done. A person entered into the bath on one side by descending down some steps. The divider indicates that a person would go down one side and come out the other. Pilgrims would have taken off their clothes before entering the water and, once in the water, they would fully immerse. Coming out on the other side they would be given a white linen robe that they would wear to the Temple. Interestingly, this description of a ritual bath and clothing in a white garment looks a lot like the Sacrament of Baptism. It also coincides perfectly with the image of taking off our old garments and putting on new ones—and of putting off the old Adam and putting on the new Adam, as Paul tells us in his Letter to the Colossians. When I'm leading a tour group to Jerusalem, I always like to stand on the southern steps of the Temple and point out the *mikvaot*, and say this is where Peter baptized the three thousand—and this was where the Church was born on Pentecost.

The Gift of the Holy Spirit

One of the primary effects of Baptism is the reception of the Holy Spirit. In the Acts of the Apostles, Peter describes the reception of the Holy Spirit as the promise of the Father. In speaking of the "promise of the Father," he was referring to Luke's Gospel where Jesus taught his disciples how to pray. After giving them the Lord's Prayer, or the *Our Father*, Jesus compared our heavenly Father to an earthly father, saying that no father would give his son a serpent if he asked for a fish, or a scorpion if he asked for an egg (*cf.* Lk 11:12). Jesus then said, "If you then, who are evil, know how to give good gifts to your children, how much more will the heavenly Father give the Holy Spirit to those who ask him!" (Lk 11:13).

Before this, Jesus had told his disciples, "Ask, and it will be given you; seek, and you will find; knock, and it will be opened to you. For every one who asks receives, and he who seeks finds, and to him who knocks it will be opened" (Lk 11:9–10). This is the key. Today, especially in the United States, we often hear a false gospel that tells us God will give us health and wealth if only we ask for it. But we know that that is not true. We may ask for health and wealth but sometimes get neither. Paul understood this. He asked God several times to remove a thorn from his flesh but his petition was never granted (*cf.* 2 Cor 12:7–9). This wasn't because Paul lacked faith, rather it wasn't God's will that the thorn be removed.

But at Pentecost we see the promise that Peter and Jesus were talking about. God promises us one thing. If you ask for the Holy Spirit, if you ask for grace—the divine life of God—it will always be given to you. God may not give you a new car or perfect health, but he will give you something far more precious and eternal and lasting, and that is his own life. He will give you the gift of the Holy Spirit.

Jesus promised the gift of the Father, which is the Holy Spirit. Immediately before he ascended into Heaven, he reminded the disciples, "You are witnesses of these things. And behold, I send the promise of my Father upon you; but stay in the city, until you are clothed with power from on high" (Lk 24:48). This refers to the coming of the Holy Spirit at Pentecost. So Jesus was going to ascend to Heaven where he will be seated at the right hand of the Father, and from where he will intercede before the Father on our behalf for the gift of the Spirit. This is exactly what Peter told his listeners in Acts. "Being therefore exalted at the right hand of God, and having received from the Father the promise of the Holy Spirit, he has poured out this which you see and hear" (Acts 2:33).

For Peter, the key is that Jesus is at the right hand of the Father. Jesus had received the promise of the Father and is now pouring out the Holy Spirit upon us. There are two key things here. First, don't underestimate the promise of the Father. The Father will always give you the gift of his Spirit, his love, his divine life, his grace. He will give you the grace that you need, if you ask for it. He will give you his own Spirit, if you ask for it. That is the promise of the Father, and it is both powerful and invaluable.

Secondly, Jesus is enthroned at the right hand of the Father right now, so when we pray to Jesus, we should pray with the confidence that he will grant us what we need. This explains Peter's confidence and boldness, which we see time and again. A few chapters later, Peter was brought before the Sanhedrin for questioning.

> On the next day their rulers and elders and scribes were gathered together in Jerusalem, with Annas the high priest and Cai'aphas and John and Alexander, and all who were of the high-priestly family. And when they had set them in the midst, they inquired, "By what power or by what name did you do this?" (Acts 4:5–7)

Peter had just healed a man who had been crippled from birth. This man had sat in front of the Temple begging for forty years. Everyone in Jerusalem knew him.

> Then Peter, filled with the Holy Spirit, said to them, "Rulers of the people and elders, if we are being examined today concerning a good deed done to a cripple, by what means this man has been healed, be it known to you all, and to all the people of Israel, that by the name of Jesus Christ of Nazareth, whom you crucified, whom God raised from the dead, by him this man is standing before you well. This is the stone which was rejected by you builders, but which has become the cornerstone. And there is salvation in no one else, for there is no other name under heaven given among men by which we must be saved." (Acts 4:8–12)

When he spoke of the stone rejected by the builders, Peter was quoting Psalm 118:22. This also relates to Jesus's parable about the vineyard and the wicked tenants. Jesus had been rejected but has become the cornerstone, and there is salvation in no one else. When the members of the Sanhedrin saw the boldness of Peter, they were taken aback. What a remarkable change in this man who had been so intimidated by a maid servant that he denied Christ three times!

Now, following the Resurrection, Ascension, and the coming of the Holy Spirit at Pentecost, Peter stood before the entire high-priestly family and all of the leading elders and boldly proclaimed Jesus Christ and boldly charged them of their guilt and sin. In fact, Peter was so bold that they were amazed (*cf.* Acts 4:13). Peter had been transformed by the promise of the Father, the gift of the Holy Spirit. That's the gift that we must ask for if we are going to be faithful disciples on the journey. Let us pray that we may be strengthened by the gifts of the Holy Spirit so that we, like Peter, can boldly witness the love of Jesus to the world for the salvation of souls.

Chapter 9

Peter Bar-Jonah:
How Peter Came to Rome

In this chapter, we'll continue our study of Peter by look-ing at his great deeds that helped found a new Christian civilization—this new city of God, as St. Augustine called it. The key moment for Peter comes in the tenth chapter of the Acts of the Apostles. Following the initial outpouring of the Holy Spirit at Pentecost and the Baptism of three thousand people, the Church in Jerusalem continued to grow. In fact, the Sanhedrin became alarmed and tried to stop this grow-ing movement by putting Peter on trial, but even they were amazed at Peter's boldness in witnessing for Christ. Peter was to be arrested again and even beaten for proclaiming Christ.

Although Peter suffered for his faith in Christ, this didn't stop his proclamation of the Gospel. Rather, his miraculous deeds climaxed in the ninth chapter of Acts, when he raised a woman named Tabitha from the dead. Tabitha was known for her works of mercy. Beloved by her friends, the Christian community in Joppa wept when she died. Peter, who was in the area, went and prayed over her and then raised her from the dead. This miracle intensified the persecution of Peter. When Jesus raised Lazarus from the dead, he became a real threat to the Jewish authorities, who then plotted to kill him. In a like manner, these miracles of Peter were winning over many to faith in Jesus, which made him a new threat to the religious authorities.

After raising Tabitha from the dead, Peter left Joppa and traveled further up the coast to the town of Caesarea Maritima. This was the great port city dedicated to Caesar Augustus, which Herod the Great built between 22 BC and 2 BC. Its man-made port made it one of the great architectural achievements of the first century. To build the port, Herod made concrete by placing large amounts of volcanic ash and rock on barges, which he floated into the harbor and sank. The mixture immediately turned into hydraulic concrete, which was resistant to salt water. In this way, he slowly built a large inner port with an outer harbor. Caesarea Maritima was ideally located as a trade juncture between the East and the West, and, in a short time, it became the busiest port in the Mediterranean. This meant that it was also the busiest port in the entire Roman Empire.

The Vision of Cornelius

"At Caesare'a there was a man named Cornelius, a centurion of what was known as the Italian Cohort" (Acts 10:1). The fact that Rome stationed its own troops in Caesarea Maritima, instead of allowing the port to be guarded by mercenaries or even soldiers from other Roman provinces, indicates the economic and strategic importance of the port to the Roman Empire. Adding to its prestige was the fact that the Roman governor, Pontius Pilate, lived Caesarea Maritima. In fact, Pilate stayed there almost exclusively, coming down to Jerusalem only on the major Jewish feast days.

Luke tells us that Cornelius was "a devout man who feared God with all his household, gave alms liberally to the people, and prayed constantly to God" (Acts 10:2). "A devout man who feared God" is a Lucan phrase meaning "God-fearer," a term used to describe Gentile men who, although not circumcised, observed Jewish customs and morality, and oftentimes even followed the Jewish dietary or kosher laws. Cornelius, who is described as pious, fell into this category of Gentiles, as did his household. The fact that he gave alms indicates that he probably came from the equestrian class, meaning that he was a wealthy Roman. Most likely, he became a "God-fearer" in Rome, which had a sizable Jewish population at the time, and specifically requested a commission to serve in Caesarea Maritima so that he and his entire household could be close to the holy sites of Israel. As a God-fearer, Cornelius naturally would have wanted to be near the birthplace of Abraham, Isaac, Jacob, and David, as well as the Temple in Jerusalem.

> About the ninth hour of the day he saw clearly in a vision an angel of God coming in and saying to him, "Cornelius." And he stared at him in terror, and said, "What is it, Lord?" And he said to him, "Your prayers and your alms have ascended as a memorial before God. And now send men to Joppa, and bring one Simon who is called Peter; he is lodging with Simon, a tanner, whose house is by the seaside." When the angel who spoke to him had departed, he called two of his servants and a devout soldier from among those that waited on him, and having related everything to them, he sent them to Joppa. (Acts 10:3–8)

Here we see that at least one of Cornelius's soldiers in his cohort—meaning one of his closest aides—was a fellow God-fearer.

The Vision of Peter

"The next day, as they were on their journey and coming near the city, Peter went up on the housetop to pray, about the sixth hour" (Acts 10:9). As we saw in an earlier chapter, the roofs of Jewish homes were normally flat, and there were steps that led to the roof where things could be stored. It was also common to go up on the roof to catch the breeze in the heat of the day. Luke tells us that Peter went up to the roof about the sixth hour, which would have been noon.

"And he became hungry and desired something to eat; but while they were preparing it, he fell into a trance and saw the heaven opened, and something descending, like a great sheet, let down by four corners upon the earth" (Acts 10:10–11). The Greek word translated here as "great sheet" is *othone*. This word was commonly used to describe a sail. Remember that Peter was a fisherman and that he is currently near the coast of Joppa.

> In [the sheet] were all kinds of animals and reptiles and birds of the air. And there came a voice to him, "Rise, Peter; kill and eat." But Peter said, "No, Lord; for I have never eaten anything that is common or unclean." And the voice came to him again a second time, "What God has cleansed, you must not call common." This happened three times, and the thing was taken up at once to heaven. (Acts 10:12–16)

The Lord is telling Peter not to call these animals unclean or unkosher but rather to kill and eat them. As an observant Jew, Peter would have found this very troubling. However, the idea of abolishing kosher dietary restrictions is an interesting pre-emptive strike by God for what is about to happen next—the messengers of Cornelius the Gentile are going to come knocking on the door of Simon the tanner and ask for Peter. Why didn't God just tell Peter to let the Gentiles come in? Why did God tell Peter to change the Jewish dietary laws first? The whole purpose of the kosher laws was to separate Israel from the Gentiles. In fact, these laws were only given to the Israelites after their exodus from Egypt, when the people were tired of eating manna and longing to eat the meat that they had enjoyed in Egypt. Under the covenants with Noah and Abraham, the Israelites could eat pork. It was only with Moses that God gave them the kosher laws.

Moses Maimonides, the great rabbi of the early Middle Ages who was quoted by St. Thomas Aquinas, gives an explanation for the kosher laws in *The Guide for the Perplexed*—a guide that could have been subtitled "For Those Who Read Leviticus." Moses Maimonides said that God gave the Israelites dietary laws to completely separate them from Egypt because they desired to go back to Egypt to eat the meat to which they had grown accustomed. Excavations near the pyramids have shown that one of the staple meats of the Egyptians was pork. Basically, God was telling the Israelites that since they wanted to go back to Egypt to eat pork, then pork was prohibited. God cut them off from what they desired in Egypt.

In the Promised Land, the kosher laws were a strategy to keep the Israelites separate from the Gentile nations. If the Israelites weren't allowed to eat with the Gentiles, then they wouldn't be tempted to attend their pagan feasts, where the prohibited meats were sacrificed to idols and then eaten by the people.

In Peter's vision, God removed that which formerly had separated the Jews from the Gentiles, and he does so to bring about unity. This prepared the way for the Gentiles' encounter with Peter.

> Now while Peter was inwardly perplexed as to what the vision which he had seen might mean, behold, the men that were sent by Cornelius, having made inquiry for Simon's house, stood before the gate and called out to ask whether Simon who was called Peter was lodging there. And while Peter was pondering the vision, the Spirit said to him, "Behold, three men are looking for you. Rise and go down, and accompany them without hesitation; for I have sent them." (Acts 10:17–20)

Seeing the three Gentiles—two servants and a soldier— would have been disquieting to Peter. But he obeyed.

> And Peter went down to the men and said, "I am the one you are looking for; what is the reason for your coming?" And they said, "Cornelius, a centurion, an upright and God-fearing man, who is well spoken of by the whole Jewish nation, was directed by a holy angel to send for you to come to his house, and to hear what you have to say." So he called them in to be his guests. The next day he rose and went off with them, and some of the brethren from Joppa accompanied him. And on the following day they entered Caesare'a.

> Cornelius was expecting them and had called together his kinsmen
> and close friends. (Acts 10:21–24)

Together, Peter and the three Gentiles traveled to Caesarea Maritima, the great city of Roman authority in the Holy Land. Cornelius, who was expecting them, had called together his kinsmen and close friends. Notice the generosity of Cornelius. He shared alms with the poor and shared his faith with family and friends. This is a great example of how to evangelize. Sometimes we get the mistaken idea that evangelization takes place in foreign parts of the world, but the New Testament shows us that evangelization always begins with family and friends and only then moves outward.

Baptism and the Gentiles

Cornelius is also important because he and his family will be the first Gentiles to receive the Sacrament of Baptism, thus becoming the first Gentiles to enter into the New Covenant established by Christ. This is a watershed moment in the history of the Church and in the story of Peter.

> When Peter entered, Cornelius met him and fell down at his feet
> and worshiped him. But Peter lifted him up, saying, "Stand up; I
> too am a man." And as he talked with him, he went in and found
> many persons gathered; and he said to them, "You yourselves know
> how unlawful it is for a Jew to associate with or to visit any one of
> another nation; but God has shown me that I should not call any
> man common or unclean. So when I was sent for, I came without
> objection. I ask then why you sent for me." (Acts 10:25–29)

Notice that Peter's vision about food no longer being unclean became a symbol for Gentiles no longer being unclean. This is highly significant as Jews believed Gentiles were defiled by unkosher or unclean food. From a Jewish perspective, unclean food made the Gentiles barbaric, or less human. An example of this can be seen in Daniel's vision of "one like a son of man" and four beasts representing the Gentile nations. The son of man is the *ben Adam* or the true son of Adam, which represents the people of Israel. The idea was that Israel was the true humanity, and the Gentiles were somewhat less than human or even animal-like.

After the vision Peter went through a great paradigm shift. His revelation taught him that there is no such thing as unclean food, and, therefore, there is no such thing as an unclean people.

> And Cornelius said, "Four days ago, about this hour, I was keeping the ninth hour of prayer in my house; and behold, a man stood before me in bright apparel, saying, 'Cornelius, your prayer has been heard and your alms have been remembered before God. Send therefore to Joppa and ask for Simon who is called Peter; he is lodging in the house of Simon, a tanner, by the seaside.' So I sent to you at once, and you have been kind enough to come. Now therefore we are all here present in the sight of God, to hear all that you have been commanded by the Lord." (Acts 10:30–33)

Just as Jesus opened his mouth to teach in the Sermon on the Mount, Peter opened his mouth to teach. "And Peter opened his mouth and said: 'Truly I perceive that God shows no partiality, but in every nation any one who fears him and does what is right is acceptable to him. You know the word which he sent to the sons of Israel, preaching good news of peace by Jesus Christ (he is Lord of all)'" (Acts 10:34–36). "Lord of all" was a title given to Caesar. Peter, in front of a very Roman audience comprised of at least one Roman officer, several Roman soldiers, and Roman aristocrats, proclaimed that it is not Caesar but Jesus of Nazareth who is "Lord of all." The boldness of his statement is profound.

"God anointed Jesus of Nazareth with the Holy Spirit and with power" (Acts 10:38). Just as he did in his homily on Pentecost day, Peter went all the way back to the very beginning, starting with the baptism of Jesus by John the Baptist. Peter viewed Jesus's baptism in the River Jordan as a kingly anointing. In the Old Testament, the prophet Samuel anointed David as the future king of Israel. In the New, the prophet John the Baptist anointed Jesus as the New David. You can see how Peter interpreted the life of Jesus in light of the kingdom, and you can see the strong undertones of the Davidic kingdom and covenant. Peter went on to teach:

> "How [Jesus] went about doing good and healing all that were oppressed by the devil, for God was with him. And we are witnesses to all that he did both in the country of the Jews and in Jerusalem. They put him to death by hanging him on a tree; but God raised him on the third day and made him manifest; not to all the people but to us who were chosen by God as witnesses, who ate and drank with him after he rose from the dead." (Acts 10:38–41)

This last verse, where he speaks of the witnesses "who ate and drank with him" after his Resurrection, has special significance when we consider what happened on the road to Emmaus and in the Upper Room when Jesus ate and drank with his disciples. Peter referred to these events to show that Jesus was not simply an apparition or a ghost but that his Resurrection was a true bodily resurrection. While many people had claimed to see ghosts or apparitions, no one had ever claimed to see a person physically risen from the dead with a glorified body, capable of eating and drinking.

> "And he commanded us to preach to the people, and to testify that he is the one ordained by God to be judge of the living and the dead. To him all the prophets bear witness that every one who believes in him receives forgiveness of sins through his name." (Acts 10:42–43)

Every time that Peter preaches in the Acts of the Apostles, he always goes back to the theme of the forgiveness of sins. This is part of the *euangelion*, or the Good News.

> While Peter was still saying this, the Holy Spirit fell on all who heard the word. And the believers from among the circumcised who came with Peter were amazed, because the gift of the Holy Spirit had been poured out even on the Gentiles. (Acts 10:44–45)

It's important to understand what this would have meant for the Jews. As Christians, we are accustomed to hearing about the Holy Spirit being in our lives and how we are strengthened through the gifts of the Holy Spirit, especially in the Sacraments of Baptism and Confirmation. In the Old Testament, however, the Holy Spirit resided in the Temple, specifically in the Holy of Holies. They understood that the place where God dwells is made holy. Therefore, the Temple was holy, and even the city of Jerusalem was holy. Because of the holiness of God and the unworthiness of man, there were all sorts of barriers to prevent people from coming close to the Spirit. For example, when Moses encountered the burning bush, we are told that he had to take off his sandals because he was standing on holy ground. He was in the presence of God. Or, if a person were ritually unclean, the Mosaic Law prohibited him or her from entering the Temple. Thus, the idea that the Holy Spirit could come and dwell in a person as if he or she were a temple was unthinkable.

At Pentecost, the Holy Spirit was poured out upon the Jewish followers of Christ in Jerusalem. Now he is poured out upon the Gentiles in Caesarea Maritima. In a sense, this is the Gentile Pentecost. It also was proof from God that Peter correctly understood the meaning of the vision. There was no longer a distinction between clean and unclean food—or between clean and unclean peoples. The Holy Spirit would rest on Gentiles, just as he had on Jews.

> For they heard them speaking in tongues and extolling God. Then Peter declared, "Can any one forbid water for baptizing these people who have received the Holy Spirit just as we have?" And he commanded them to be baptized in the name of Jesus Christ. Then they asked him to remain for some days. (Acts 10:46–48)

Just as he did at Pentecost, Peter baptized. It's interesting how focused Peter was on the Sacrament of Baptism. If you go back and read the First Letter of Peter, he talks about being born anew, or being born from on high, not with perishable seed but with imperishable seed. Thus, Baptism was central to Peter's teaching as well as the idea of sanctuary, temple, and Holy Spirit. Peter told his readers that we are to be living stones and priests to offer up ourselves as a living sacrifice. This imagery of the Temple makes perfect sense when we consider the Jewish understanding that the Spirit of God dwelt in the Temple. Thus, the Holy Spirit, who now dwells in us through Baptism, makes us temples of God. We are the living stones of the great temple that Jesus is building—the Church. We see all of this in Peter's preaching to Cornelius and company.

A tremendous controversy ensued when the people of Jerusalem found out that Peter ate with Gentiles and even baptized them. But Peter gave testimony that he did so based on God's revelation to him. "When they heard this they were silenced. And they glorified God, saying, 'Then to the Gentiles also God has granted repentance unto life'" (Acts 11:18).

Peter and Jonah

The fact that Peter's vision happened in Joppa is also highly significant. Joppa was an ancient port that is mentioned only one time in the entirety of the Old Testament—in the story of Jonah the prophet—which provides a backdrop to what happens here with Peter. God asked Jonah, who was from the northern kingdom of Israel, to go to Nineveh, the capital of Assyria, to preach to the people living there. He was to tell the people of Nineveh that unless they repented, God would smite their city. When God summoned Jonah to go east to Nineveh, however, Jonah immediately turned and went west to Joppa. There, he got in a ship that was manned by Gentiles and planned to sail as far as he possibly could from Nineveh. The reason he didn't want to go to Nineveh was that it was the archenemy of Israel, and there was a constant tension and conflict between the two. In fact, Jonah would have been quite happy if God actually did smite Nineveh.

The story continues with God sending a storm to keep Jonah from leaving, yet Jonah still goes on. Eventually, the storms intensify to the extent that the sailors feared the ship would sink. Jonah knew it was God who was causing the tempest to prevent him from running away, so he told the sailors to throw him overboard. Jonah hated Nineveh so much that he would rather drown than go back and preach to the people there. But God was going to change Jonah's heart in a powerful way. When the sailors threw Jonah overboard, he was swallowed by a big fish that brought him back to Israel. Jonah repented, but only partially. He went to Nineveh and told the people that they had to repent. Ironically, Jonah's preaching worked a miraculous conversion among the people in Nineveh—something that he couldn't achieve among the ten tribes of northern Israel.

Whereas Jonah fled to Joppa in the Old Testament, it was here in Joppa where Peter first heard about Gentiles being included among the people of God. The parallel between Peter and Jonah is that Peter, who was from Zebulon and Naphtali, just like Jonah, would end up taking a ship with Gentiles from Caesarea Maritima so far west that he ended up in Rome. Like Jonah preaching in Nineveh, Peter would preach in Rome, the current archenemy of Israel, in the adversary's own city. And, as with Jonah, Peter's preaching would be received with repentance and acceptance—so much so that it sowed the seeds for the eventual conversion of the Roman Empire. When you look at their respective stories in this light, you can see that Peter and Jonah had a lot in common.

This story of Jonah also reminds us of Christ's prophecy from the sixteenth chapter of Matthew. The Pharisees and Sadducees asked Jesus to give them a sign, but he told them that no sign would be given to that evil and adulterous generation, except the "sign of Jonah." Later that day, Jesus and his disciples went to Caesarea Philippi where Peter professed faith in Jesus, and Jesus said, "Blessed are you, Simon Bar-Jona" (Mt 16:17). In other words, Peter is "Bar-Jonah" because he is the disciple, or spiritual son, in the prophetic line of Jonah. The reason Jesus changed Peter's surname is that he intended all along for Peter to go to Rome and preach to the Gentiles, just like Jonah had been sent to the people of Nineveh. All of this was foreordained and planned by Jesus. It's amazing to consider how Divine Providence orders things to bring about God's plan of salvation.

Persecution

Beginning in Chapter 12, the story begins to darken for Peter and the Christians in Jerusalem. "About that time Herod the king laid violent hands upon some who belonged to the Church. He killed James the brother of John with the sword; and when he saw that it pleased the Jews, he proceeded to arrest Peter also" (Acts 12:1–3). This probably occurred around AD 41–42 when Herod Agrippa took power and was appointed by Rome as the successor of Herod Antipater, thus becoming the leader of the Herodian dynasty. "This was during the days of Unleavened Bread" (Acts 12:3). Luke mentions the "days of Unleavened Bread" to show us how the life of Peter paralleled the life of Christ. For example, Jesus raised Lazarus from the dead, and then Peter raised Tabitha from the dead. Jesus had been arrested and crucified during the previous Passover. Here, during the next Passover, we see the arrest of Peter.

"And when he had seized him, he put him in prison, and delivered him to four squads of soldiers to guard him, intending after the Passover to bring him out to the people" (Acts 12:4). In the case of Jesus, the Pharisees, scribes, and chief priest conspired to have him killed, but not during the Passover "lest there be a tumult among the people" (Mt 26:5). Likewise, Herod didn't want to kill Peter during the Passover as that would be politically dangerous. So Peter was kept in prison. The Christian community prayed earnestly for him and for his release—a prayer that would be answered by God in dramatic fashion.

As the leader of this new Christian movement, Peter was considered dangerous, and he had already escaped from the Sanhedrin once before, so Herod wasn't taking any chances. He assigned four squads of soldiers to watch him. That night, Peter was sleeping between two soldiers. He was bound in chains and two sentries were guarding the door. Under Roman law, if a prisoner escaped during a soldier's watch, then the soldier would be executed. This is important as no one would ever claim that four squads of Roman soldiers had been bribed to release Peter. What soldier—much less four squads—would ever take money knowing that he surely would be executed?

When I consider this story, I am reminded of Raphael's painting *The Deliverance of St. Peter*, which hangs in the Vatican Museum. The painting's lighting is particularly interesting. Outside the prison you see a moonlit sky with dawn breaking just over the horizon. Near the cell of Peter, a guard's torch throws up some light as well. But the main source of illumination is the brilliant light radiating from the liberating angel. So you have several plays on light—the light of the torch, the light of the moon, and the light of the early dawn—but the light of God makes the others pale in comparison. This makes me think of 1 Peter 2:9, when Peter says, "[God] called you out of darkness into his marvelous light."

The angel appeared in the cell, woke Peter, and told him to get up quickly, and the chains miraculously fell off Peter's hands. Then the angel told Peter to dress, put on his sandals, wrap himself in his cloak, and to follow him. Although Peter thought the angel was a vision, he obeyed. It was only after he was led out of the prison and the angel disappeared that he realized that the angel was real.

Interestingly, Raphael paints the features of Peter according to the traditional depiction but with a twist. He includes some features of Pope Julius II, then the reigning pontiff. Raphael places these features on Peter to show that the papacy may be enclosed in darkness and persecution but God's light will always lead the successors of Peter.

The Deliverance of St. Peter by Raphael

After his miraculous escape from prison, Peter went to the house of Mary, the mother of John. John was also known by his Greco-Roman name Mark, and sometimes the two names were combined to form John Mark. He is best known as the author of the Gospel that bears his name, and he is the same person whom Peter will refer to as "my son Mark" (1 Pt 5:13) in his first epistle. Many of the Christians had gathered there in the house to pray for Peter, and, when Peter knocked, the maid Rhoda came to the door. She recognized Peter's voice but was so excited that she ran to tell the others instead of letting him in. However, no one would believe her. Rather, they thought she was imagining things or perhaps it was an angel that had appeared. Peter kept knocking, though, and eventually the door was opened. Only then, when they saw him in person, did they come to believe.

> Now when day came, there was no small stir among the soldiers
> over what had become of Peter. And when Herod had sought for
> him and could not find him, he examined the sentries and ordered
> that they should be put to death. Then he went down from Judea to
> Caesare'a, and remained there. (Acts 12:18–19)

Herod was looking for Peter, so Peter went to Caesarea. Herod Agrippa had dominion in Galilee and was staying in Jerusalem at the time. But he didn't have jurisdiction in Caesarea, which was under Roman jurisdiction. Additionally, Peter had a powerful friend there—Cornelius, whom he had just baptized. You can see Divine Providence at work here. It is at this point that Peter disappears from the story of Acts. Luke tells us that Peter went to another place, but he doesn't say where. Of course, we know that Peter went to Rome, but it would have been too dangerous for Luke to publicize where Peter was currently staying.

Peter's Story Continues through Tradition

Tradition, however, picks up where the Scriptures leave off. According to Tradition, Peter went to Rome around AD 42, and, in a wonderful example of how Scripture and Tradition fit together beautifully, Luke may have given us a clue as to how he went there. Peter knew Cornelius, the Roman centurion, who was from the unit called the Italian Cohort. When Peter went to Caesarea, he was in danger of death, and so it is reasonable to believe that Cornelius helped him to escape from Herod Agrippa's territory. As mentioned before, Cornelius was from Rome and probably was already a God-fearer before he came to Caesarea. If so, he would have known other God-fearers in Rome who were sympathetic to Judaism, so he could have arranged for Peter to stay with family or friends in Rome.

Tradition tells us that when Peter went to Rome he was hosted by Pudens, who was one of the four hundred Roman senators. Although Tradition doesn't tell us how Peter came to know Pudens, we can speculate that Pudens was a friend of Cornelius. Both were Roman aristocrats, and both were God-fearers. Cornelius could have written a letter of introduction to Senator Pudens.

As if in confirmation of this theory, there is a church in Rome named after St. Pudenziana, the daughter of Senator Pudens. Pudenziana and her sister Prassede are known for their heroism in burying Christian martyrs who were killed during the persecution of Caesar Nero. If you go underneath the church to the cavity below, you can see the ruins of Senator Pudens' home, and archaeologists have discovered a brick dated to the first century that is stamped with his name. Even more curiously, the Church of St. Pudenziana has an ancient Roman bath that was converted into a baptistery. This alone doesn't prove that Pudens was a Christian, but it is evidence that this was the site of his home.

Further evidence, however, can be found in Scripture. Second Timothy was written by Paul when he was in prison in Rome. In this letter, he tells Timothy, "Eubu'lus sends greetings to you, as do Pudens and Linus and Claudia and all the brethren" (2 Tm 4:21). Pudens is listed right next to Linus, another Roman aristocrat who had a house large enough to host the nascent Church in Rome—and it is this Linus who will become the successor to Peter.

The Church of St. Pudenziana has a mosaic that dates to AD 390, which makes it the oldest mosaic found in any church in Rome. The mosaic depicts the Twelve Apostles with Jesus, and another depiction shows Pudens being baptized by Peter. It's curious that the Apostles are wearing Roman senatorial togas, and, in the background, there are buildings in the Holy Land that were built by Emperor Constantine's mother, St. Helena, earlier that century. The Christian who made this mosaic probably had visited the Holy Land. Thus the church serves as a bridge between Jerusalem and Rome—a connection that must have its origin in the fact that Peter was hosted here.

Another fascinating aspect of the Church of St. Pudenziana is that a Eucharistic miracle happened on one of its side altars. During the Protestant Reformation, a priest was losing his faith in the Real Presence of Christ in the Eucharist. While celebrating Mass, he dropped a consecrated host, which fell on the marble steps of the altar. Upon hitting the ground, the host caught on fire and burned its imprint into the marble, which you still can see today. This miracle bolstered the priest's flagging faith more powerfully than any theological argument, converting him into a real believer in the Real Presence. It seems especially fitting that God worked a Eucharistic miracle at a church housing an altar upon which Peter himself celebrated Mass.

In the next chapter, we will continue our study of Peter in Rome. Let us thank God for his Divine Providence and ask that he help us trust in his plan for us and for his Church. Let us ask him to guide us just as he guided Peter, so that we can go forward with the faith of Peter and with the boldness that comes from knowing that God has a plan for our lives and will supply all of our needs.

Chapter 10

Quo Vadis: *Peter's Way of the Cross*

In this final chapter, we will look at the life of Peter predominantly through the lens of Christian Tradition. As we saw earlier, the Acts of the Apostles tells us that Peter went from Joppa to Caesarea (meaning Caesarea Maritima, an important Roman port city), where he baptized the first Gentiles. After that, he was imprisoned in Jerusalem by Herod Agrippa but escaped through a miraculous event. Then Luke tells us that Peter returned to Caesarea Maritima—but Scripture doesn't tell us more about Peter after that. It's as if Peter has disappeared from the story.

Fortunately, Tradition picks up the story where Scripture leaves off. From early Christian Tradition we learn that Peter went to Rome. In the last chapter, we speculated that Cornelius could have made the arrangements for his voyage and might have provided him with a letter of introduction to Cornelius's family or friends in Rome. Tradition tells us that, upon arriving in Rome, Peter stayed with Senator Pudens. He, like Cornelius, was a God-fearer who observed the Jewish Law. Pudens first heard the Gospel proclaimed from Peter, who later baptized him.

The Church of St. Prassede

Tradition also tells us that Pudens's home was used as a church for the early Christian community in Rome. We know that later the Church of St. Pudenziana, named in honor of one of his daughters, was built over the site. Interestingly, there is another church further up the same hill named after Pudens's other daughter, St. Prassede, which was built over the site of her home; and it is here that both sisters are buried. Both of these churches are located in the neighborhood of the Basilica of St. Mary Major.

In the last chapter, we looked at the importance of the Church of St. Pudenziana, but there is an additional fascinating aspect about this church. Behind and to the left of the church's main altar is a side altar, behind which stands a statue of Peter receiving the keys from Jesus, and under this altar, preserved in a rectangular reliquary, is half a table. It is believed that this is a table that Peter used as an altar to celebrate Mass. Why only half a table? When the Archbasilica of St. John Lateran was constructed after Constantine legalized Christianity in 313, the Church naturally wished to relocate the Petrine relic to this new cathedral in Rome. However, the early Christians who worshiped at the Church of St. Pudenziana were not eager to relinquish the relic, so they decided to divide it in half. Now, half of Peter's table is at the Church of St. Pudenziana, and the other half is at St. John Lateran.

Statue above reliquary in St. Pudenziana, Rome

Most pilgrims to Rome will visit St. Peter's Basilica to pray at the tomb of Peter or tour St. John Lateran, the pope's cathedral, which also served as the papal residence for nearly a thousand years. However, most travelers visiting Rome don't realize that there is a church built over the home where Peter actually lived, worked, and worshiped. In a certain regard, the humble churches of Sts. Pudenziana and Prassede more fittingly represent the simple fisherman from Galilee.

I mention these early Church Traditions to reinforce how valuable they are to the Christian story—our story—and how they fit so well with Scripture. As Catholics, it is important to know the origin of our story—a story that is based not only in Scripture and Sacred Tradition but also in the Church's tradition. As a Church, we find ourselves at another critical moment in history. All of the recent popes have urgently called us to the New Evangelization, which will lead to a new springtime for the Church. This New Evangelization is also an invitation to return to our origins. Only when we understand our own story and see how it comes together will we be able to share that story with others. This witness to which we are called is indispensable to renewing the Church.

Quo Vadis

In Chapter 4, we saw how Jesus brought the disciples to Caesarea Philippi, and how Peter, in plain view of the temple dedicated to Caesar Augustus, proclaimed his faith in Jesus as the true "son of the living God," the true Messiah, and the true King. Jesus intentionally prompted Peter's profession of faith here, in this particular setting, because it represented the primary challenge that Peter would face in his mission: how to preach the Gospel in a Roman world that worshiped the emperor as a god. Peter's profession of faith prepared him for his mission as the "Bar-Jonah." Later, after Pentecost, Jesus revealed to Peter that Gentiles were to be included in the New Covenant that he established. Departing Caesarea Maritima, Peter would go to the heart of the Roman Empire and preach the Good News and call the people to repentance. In time, many of the people in Rome would convert, and Peter, along with Paul, would eventually become the patron saints of the city.

The Appian Way of the Cross

On July 19 of AD 64, a terrible fire ravaged ten out of the fourteen regions of the city of Rome. Rumor began to spread that the emperor Nero was behind the fire, and he needed a scapegoat to blame as backlash was quickly building against him. He blamed the Christians and quickly focused all the might of Rome upon one goal—a most public and ruthless hunting down and execution of any and all Christians.

Fearing for Peter's life, the Christians in Rome told him that he needed to flee the city. As a first-hand witness to the life and teachings of Christ, and as the leader of the Church, Peter was important to the Christian community. Listening to the people, Peter left Rome by a road called the Appian Way. To this day, you can walk the same well-worn stones of this famous road. While Peter was walking down the Appian Way, he saw someone coming. The person was bent over and carrying a heavy burden. As the person approached, Peter realized that it was Jesus, carrying the Cross. Peter went up to Jesus and asked, *"Domine, quo vadis?"* ("Lord, where are you going?"). Jesus responded, "I am going to Rome to be crucified once again." The *Via Dolorosa* now merged into the *Via Appia*.

Basically, Jesus was telling Peter that he was abandoning his flock in their hour of need and that he should go back to suffer along with them. If not, Christ would go himself. This reminds us of Jesus's words at the Last Supper when he told Peter, "When you have turned again, strengthen your brethren" (Lk 22:32). It also reminds us of Caesarea Philippi when Jesus told his disciples that he must go to Jerusalem to be crucified. Peter told him, "God forbid, Lord!" (Mt 16:22), and was soundly rebuked by Jesus. After the Resurrection, Peter had learned "the way of the Cross" in the trials and persecution he endured. He had learned through experience the redemptive value of suffering, which is an embrace of God's will and an expression of one's gift of self. Love given in sacrifice can never undermine God's plan.

Located outside the old gates of the city, where Peter would have left Rome by the Appian Way, there is a small, humble church popularly known as the Church of Domine Quo Vadis. Tradition has it that Jesus left two footprints on the stone where he stood when he encountered Peter on the Appian Way. That stone bearing Christ's alleged footprints is not on public display—it is kept nearby in the sanctuary of the Basilica of St. Sebastian Outside the Walls—but there is a replica that you can see inside the center of the Church of Domine Quo Vadis.

Following his encounter with Christ, Peter immediately turned around and headed back to Rome where he would strengthen the community and prepare them for martyrdom—leading the way with his own. The story of *Quo Vadis* is a beautiful part of Christian Tradition that was passed on orally for a brief time but was already found in written form by the second century AD (e.g. *The Acts of Peter*). There is a stunning painting by Annibale Carracci that depicts this scene in the life of Peter. Aside from the *Quo Vadis* Tradition, there are numerous other testimonials of Peter's death in Rome that were written down and often referred to by Church Fathers such as Sts. Irenaeus and Ignatius.

The story of *Quo Vadis* was turned into a novel by the great Polish writer Henryk Sienkiewicz, who wrote about the Traditions of the early Roman Christians, their evangelization of Rome, and ultimately the martyrdom of Peter. It was such an inspiring novel that it became a best seller and was translated into more languages than any previous novel. Eventually, *Quo Vadis* made it to the big screen in a 1951 film, a classic of the biblical-epic genre so popular at the time.

The *Quo Vadis* encounter teaches us that discipleship involves conforming ourselves to the crucified Lord. Authentic discipleship is always cruciform. Its beams do not meet at the cross-section of worldly glory and success. It's never the "health and wealth" gospel. It is cruciform, and we must embrace it.

In Mark's Gospel, which is based on Peter's preaching, there is a section that details Jesus's final journey to Jerusalem. This section, which is sometimes referred to as "The Way," is bookended by the healing of two blind men: in Chapter 8, the blind man in Bethsaida, and in Chapter 10, the blind beggar, Bartimaeus. In between these two healings, Jesus predicts his Passion on three separate occasions—and three times the Apostles ignore or deny it. What's fascinating is that their blindness to Jesus's insistence that discipleship is cruciform begins and ends with the healing of a blind man. After the second healing, Jesus tells Bartimaeus that he is free to go on "his way" (Mk 10:52). But Mark tells us that Bartimaeus followed Jesus on "the way" to Jerusalem where Jesus would be crucified. The way of Jesus is the way of the Cross. Thus, the Tradition of *Quo Vadis* matches up perfectly with this section of Mark's Gospel. Again you see the alignment of Scripture and Tradition. It's all the same story. Like Jesus, Peter will go the way of the Cross.

The Cost of Discipleship

Tradition informs us that Paul, who was a Roman citizen, was beheaded, but Peter was crucified like Jesus. The event is described in another ancient writing called *The Acts of Peter*. With great humility, Peter knew that he was not worthy to die in the same manner of our Lord, and so he asked to be crucified upside down. This scene of Peter being crucified upside down was depicted in dramatic fashion in a Renaissance painting by Caravaggio, and the realism is powerful. Peter is a strong, muscular man, even in his old age. Three men are crucifying him, but the weight of his powerful frame makes it difficult for them to lift the cross. You have one man with his back bent over at the top of the cross with a rope, and it isn't clear whether the rope will be strong enough. There is another man at the middle of the cross and a third at the bottom.

Peter's Crucifixion by Caravaggio

All three are straining to raise the cross. As the sun sets, you see the light fall on Peter. This is not the typical depiction of an idealized Peter with a halo and bright colors in a majestic setting. Rather, the painting is very realistic. Caravaggio even painted Peter's bare feet with dirty bottoms. Nailed to the cross, his feet stick out at the viewer, hiding nothing of the horror he endured willingly for the Lord and his flock.

Caravaggio was commissioned to paint this depiction of Peter's crucifixion in honor of the great jubilee year that took place in 1600. He also painted a similarly powerful depiction of the conversion of Paul. The hope of that jubilee year, which followed the height of the Protestant Reformation, was to encourage pilgrimages to Rome and inspire a new evangelization that would help bring fallen-away Catholics back to the Church. For this reason, these two paintings were placed in the Basilica of Santa Maria del Popolo, a prominent church in one of the larger piazzas on the northern side of Rome near the entrance of the main road from the north. The hope was that pilgrims entering Rome from the north would stop by this church and be inspired by these dramatic paintings. It was the hope that the pilgrims, seeing the conversion of Paul and the crucifixion of Peter, would understand the importance and truth of the papacy. Peter and Paul, the patron saints of Rome, were used for outreach in the "new evangelization" focused on re-converting Catholics who had entered into Protestantism.

Before this, Michelangelo, Caravaggio's great hero and model, painted Peter and Paul together. When he had finished painting the Sistine Chapel, Michelangelo was commissioned to work on the Vatican's Pauline Chapel. On the two main walls, he painted the conversion of Paul and the crucifixion of Peter. This would have been completed nearly sixty years before Caravaggio's painting of Peter's crucifixion. In Michelangelo's painting, Peter is being lifted up in the same manner as in Caravaggio's painting. As he is being lifted up, though, he strains his neck to look at you. It's as if Peter is asking, "Are you ready to die for Christ? Are you ready to follow Jesus all the way from your Galilee to your Golgotha? Are you ready for the cost of discipleship?" That's the lesson that Peter had to learn, and that's the lesson for us today.

This "cost of discipleship" is the significance of Michelangelo's painting, which he painted at the height of the Reformation. Michelangelo knew the Pauline Chapel was used by the popes and that Mass would be offered there by the cardinals of a conclave before entering the Sistine Chapel to elect a new successor to Peter. The cardinals would, and unto this day can, look out and see Peter, craning his neck in pain, stretched out on the cross, looking at them as if to say, "Which one of *you* wants to be pope? Are you ready to be a good shepherd, even if it means dying for your flock? Because this is where it could lead."

Although the Pauline Chapel is privately used only by the Holy Father and some of the cardinals, I was fortunate enough to be able to visit it the year after these paintings had been restored in 2009. After a conclave has reached a decision, the newly elected pope comes to the Pauline Chapel to pray. Here he will see the painting of the crucified Peter looking at him. Michelangelo painted it in a way that no matter where

The Crucifixion of Peter by Michelangelo

you are standing in the room, you won't be able to escape Peter's gaze. The Pauline Chapel is called the "room of tears" because the newly elected pope usually cries at the weight of his new responsibility to lead the Church.

The Suffering Shepherd

During Peter's threefold reaffirmation of his love for Jesus in John's Gospel, Jesus told him to "feed my sheep." The significance of this can be found earlier in this Gospel when Jesus said, "I am the good shepherd. The good shepherd lays down his life for the sheep" (Jn 10:11). Following Peter's threefold reaffirmation, Jesus said to him,

> "Truly, truly, I say to you, when you were young, you fastened your own belt and walked where you would; but when you are old, you will stretch out your hands, and another will fasten your belt and carry you where you do not wish to go." (This he said to show by what death he was to glorify God.) And after this he said to him, "Follow me." (Jn 21:18–19)

Jesus is the type of shepherd that lays down his life for his flock and, once he has passed the shepherd's staff to Peter, he asks Peter to be such a shepherd as well. In his first epistle, when he addresses the elders of the church communities, Peter demonstrates that he had learned this lesson: "And when the chief Shepherd is manifested you will obtain the unfading crown of glory" (1 Pt 5:4). This is Peter's admonition that a shepherd must be willing to suffer. Christ has given us the example, and Peter understood that he, too, would have to suffer for his flock.

This willingness of the shepherd to suffer for his sheep has literally been woven into the fabric of the liturgical vestments worn by popes and archbishops, who are given the pallium—a thin strip of white wool cloth with crosses on it. It is worn around the neck and shoulders in a circular fashion. We are all familiar with paintings of Jesus the Good Shepherd, which show him carrying a sheep on his shoulders. The pallium symbolizes that its wearer is a shepherd. The bearer carries his sheep, signified by the woolen strip around his neck and shoulders. The pallium also symbolizes that he must carry his cross and be prepared to give up his life for his sheep.

There are many artistic depictions of Peter wearing the pallium, probably anachronistic, since its use did not become customary for popes and metropolitan bishops until the fifth century. The pope gives the pallium to new archbishops in a very moving and beautiful ceremony on June 29, the Solemnity of Sts. Peter and Paul. It also is interesting to note that the wool for the palliums comes from sheep that are raised by the Sisters of St. Agnes (from the Latin *agnus* meaning "lamb") in the area of Rome where Paul was martyred. The sisters shear the sheep and weave the wool to make the palliums. The night before they are given to the archbishops, the palliums are placed on Peter's tomb in St. Peter's Basilica as a reminder that the archbishops are called to be good shepherds, just like Christ—and Peter.

Victors and Conquerors

Tradition tells us that Peter was martyred near Nero's private circus on the Vatican Hill—across the Tiber from the old city of Rome—and that his body was hastily buried in a nearby cemetery. After becoming emperor in the early fourth century, Constantine built a large basilica on the Vatican Hill and located its main altar directly over Peter's tomb. In the sixteenth century, the present St. Peter's Basilica was constructed in its place. Like the previous basilica, St. Peter's has its main altar directly over the tomb of Peter. When renovations were being made around the time of World War II, workers came across what appeared to be a first-century tomb. Suspecting it to be Peter's, permission was obtained from Pope Pius XII to begin excavations to ascertain that Peter was actually buried there. Permission was given, but the excavations had to be kept secret as Pius XII was worried the Nazis would occupy the Vatican at any moment. Hitler, who was virtually obsessed by the occult, might have tried to steal the relics of Peter. To avoid detection, the dirt the workers removed was secretly deposited in the Vatican gardens.

The excavations revealed a tomb right under the main altar of St. Peter's Basilica. When the bone fragments were later analyzed and carbon dated, it was determined that they belonged to a first-century male. One part of the body, however, could never be located—the feet. Since Peter was crucified upside down, they most likely cut off his feet in order to remove him from the cross rather than take the effort to pry out the nail. Early Christians then buried the rest of the body, which would explain why Peter was entombed footless.

The excavations also found graffiti on the tomb that included paintings of palm branches, which symbolize victory. This is evidence of the Christian belief that martyrs are victorious. In the Book of Revelation, we read about the martyrs who wear robes that are made white by the blood of the Lamb—and these martyrs are carrying palm branches. The graffiti also included the Greek word *nikao*, a verb meaning to "conquer" or "prevail," which comes from the noun *nike*, meaning "victory." In the case of Peter, the palm branches and the word *nikao* are indications that he was victorious and was therefore going to receive the crown of victory. This also reminds us of something Peter wrote to the early Church: "And when the chief Shepherd is manifested you will obtain the unfading crown of glory" (1 Pt 5:4). This also reminds us of what Paul wrote to the church in Rome about a decade before Nero's persecution.

> If God is for us, who is against us? He who did not spare his own Son but gave him up for us all, will he not also give us all things with him? Who shall bring any charge against God's elect? It is God who justifies; who is to condemn? Is it Christ Jesus, who died, yes, who was raised from the dead, who is at the right hand of God, who indeed intercedes for us? Who shall separate us from the love of Christ? Shall tribulation, or distress, or persecution, or famine, or nakedness, or peril, or sword? As it is written,
>
> "For your sake we are being killed all the day long;
>
> we are regarded as sheep to be slaughtered."
>
> No, in all these things we are more than conquerors through him who loved us. For I am sure that neither death, nor life, nor angels, nor principalities, nor things present, nor things to come, nor powers, nor height, nor depth, nor anything else in all creation, will be able to separate us from the love of God in Christ Jesus our Lord. (Rom 8:31–39)

The point that Paul is making is that nothing, including martyrdom, can separate us from Jesus. He was truly inspired by the Holy Spirit, as he was writing these words just a few years before Nero's horrendous persecutions. Paul even uses the term "sheep for the slaughter." Here, he is quoting from the Psalms: "You have made us like sheep for slaughter" (Ps 44:11). And when Paul says that "we are more than conquerors," he uses the Greek word *nikao*.

This theme of *nikao* (to conquer) runs through the whole Book of Revelation. For example, John speaks about "he who conquers" or "to him who conquers" when writing to each of the seven churches at the beginning of his book.

- "To him who conquers I will grant to eat of the tree of life, which is in the paradise of God" (Rev 2:7).
- "He who conquers shall not be hurt by the second death" (Rev 2:11).
- "To him who conquers I will give some of the hidden manna, and I will give him a white stone, with a new name written on the stone which no one knows except him who receives it" (Rev 2:17).
- "He who conquers and who keeps my works until the end, I will give him power over the nations" (Rev 2:26).
- "He who conquers shall be clothed like them in white garments, and I will not blot his name out of the book of life; I will confess his name before my Father and before his angels" (Rev 3:5).
- "He who conquers, I will make him a pillar in the temple of my God; never shall he go out of it, and I will write on him the name of my God, and the name of the city of

my God, the new Jerusalem which comes down from my God out of heaven, and my own new name" (Rev 3:12).

- "He who conquers, I will grant him to sit with me on my throne, as I myself conquered and sat down with my Father on his throne" (Rev 3:21).

In the seventh chapter of Revelation, we see the reason for this seven-fold repetition. John has a vision of Jesus as a lamb who is slain, but the lamb conquers (*nikao*) by being slain. Peter did the same thing. He conquered by being slain for love. He conquered by love, and nothing that Satan, or Caesar, or Rome, or anyone else could have done would ever separate Peter from the love of Jesus. This is also our surety and our hope.

When we get attached to worldly things, we become anxious because we know that we can be separated from them. We can be separated from our home, from our wealth, from our car, and from our favorite possessions, but never can we be separated from the love of Jesus. And if the love of Jesus is at the center of our lives, then our anxiety will be small and short-lived. We need not fear economic downturn, famine, peril, storm, or persecution because these things cannot take away the love of Christ. When everything is in the right place, our lives are ordered. Like the early Christians, we become fearless because we are filled with the love of Christ. As we just read, Paul told the Roman Christians, "In all these things we are more than conquerors through him who loved us" (Rom 8:37).

Peter's willingness to suffer and even die for his faith goes to the veracity of his testimony. When he spoke about Jesus he must have been telling the truth because it was a truth he was willing to die for. This was the whole point of the preaching of the first Christians, many of whom actually knew Christ when he walked among them. This is truth in which we can place our trust.

Proclaiming the Good News of Jesus Christ

We will end our study of Peter by looking a final time at the new names that Jesus gave him. When I visited Peter's tomb underneath St. Peter's Basilica, it really struck me that Peter's name means "rock," and it is upon this rock that Christ built his Church. Peter's bones lie beneath all the rock upon which the foundation of the basilica is built. What a fitting symbol. The Basilica of St. Peter is literally built on Peter's bones. Symbolically—as well as actually—Peter is the rock upon which Christ builds his Church.

Jesus also changed Peter's surname to "Bar-Jonah." On the ceiling of the Sistine Chapel is Michelangelo's famous depiction of the story of Genesis. Great prophets of the Old Testament align the sides of the ceiling, while the Last Judgment is paint-ed on the wall above the main altar. Basically, Michelangelo captured the entire story of salvation from the beginning until the end, from Creation until the Last Judgment. Whenever cardinal-electors come together to choose a successor to Peter, Michelangelo wanted them to see and contemplate this grand drama unfolding all around them. He wanted them to realize that they would be judged on how they voted.

Among the many prophets that Michelangelo depicted, one is larger than the rest—Jonah, along with the figure of a large fish. Why was Jonah included, and why is he larger than the other prophets? When you look closer, you see that he is placed on one of the capitals—the upper end of a column— and it looks like he and the fish are about to fall off. If you look downward, they would fall directly on the *cathedra*, or chair, of the Holy Father. Michelangelo was a very devout man and a great student of the Bible. In particular, he studied the Scriptures in detail before painting these images. He understood that Jonah was a key symbol for Peter and that Peter and his successors, the popes, were to be "bar-Jonahs"—prophets like Jonah—entrusted with proclaiming God's message of love, mercy, and forgiveness to the world.

The Prophet Jonah by Michelangelo

Since her foundation, the Church has always been called to look outward. Peter the Galilean, like Jonah, was sent to the great capital of the world of that time, which happened to be Israel's archenemy, to proclaim the Good News of Jesus Christ. Every pope is likewise called to proclaim the Good News of repentance to the entire world. As Christians, we cannot turn inward. We must go out into the streets and proclaim the truth. Pope Francis—the successor of Peter Bar-Jonah—is calling us to do just that.

The story of Peter is our story, and it is worth retelling. It's worth telling how we go from Jesus in Galilee to the Catholic Church in Rome by following the footsteps of Jesus's greatest disciple, Peter the Galilean.

Let us pray that God will give us grace and strength so that nothing may separate us from his love. May we let go of all the things about which we are anxious, all of the things of which we are afraid, and all of the things that preoccupy our thoughts and our hearts. May God help us to understand that these things are as nothing compared to the love of Christ.

Art Credits

Sarcophagus of Sabinas in the Vatican Museum, Augustine Institute.

Rembrandt's *Storm on Sea of Galilee* / HIP / Art Resource, NY.

Pietro Perugino's *The Delivery of the Keys.*

Icon of Peter's threefold denial in St. Peter Gallicantu, Jerusalem, Augustine Institute.

Icon of Peter weeping in St. Peter Gallicantu, Jerusalem, Augustine Institute.

Icon of Peter's threefold affirmation in St. Peter Gallicantu, Jerusalem, Augustine Institute.

Raphael's *The Liberation of St. Peter from Prison* / Scala / Art Resource, NY.

Unknown artist's statue of Jesus delivering the keys to Peter in St. Pudenziana, Rome, Augustine Institute.

Caravaggio's *Peter's Crucifixion* / Scala / Art Resource, NY.

Michelangelo's *The Crucifixion of Peter* / Erich Lessing / Art Resource, NY.

Michelangelo's *The Prophet Jonah* / Erich Lessing / Art Resource, NY.